COCKTAILS FROM HELL

Also by Col. Austin Bay

Embrace the Suck
A Quick and Dirty Guide to War
From Shield to Storm
Ataturk: The Greatest General of the Ottoman Empire
Coyote Cried Twice
Prism
The Wrong Side of Brightness

FIVE COMPLEX WARS
SHAPING THE 21ST CENTURY

COCKTAILS
FROM HELL

COL. AUSTIN BAY

A BOMBARDIER BOOKS BOOK
An Imprint of Post Hill Press

Cocktails from Hell:
Five Complex Wars Shaping the 21st Century
© 2018 by Col. Austin Bay
All Rights Reserved

ISBN: 978-1-68261-661-1
ISBN (eBook): 978-1-68261-662-8

Cover Design by Christian Bentulan

Post Hill Press
New York • Nashville
posthillpress.com

Published in the United States of America

We live here. We lie in the Present's unopened
Sorrow; its limits are what we are.
The prisoner ought never to pardon his cell.

—W.H. AUDEN, from *In Time of War*

TABLE OF CONTENTS

INTRODUCTION

On an evening in February 1990, three months after the Berlin Wall cracked and the Cold War began to melt, I participated in a panel presentation held in a high school auditorium.

My memories of the panel—the evening's center ring—mix "so damn what" with the dim and the understandably forgotten. The auditorium clearly doubled as the school lunch room. The panel consisted of a moderator and three or four writers—the precise number escapes me. The moderator had told/warned us the program had a "how to develop a career" angle, so she asked each of us to briefly summarize how we acquired individual expertise in a particular subject. I recall the moderator introduced me as a defense expert and then added that I had written a critically acclaimed novel. Yes, I remember that. At one point someone asked for my take on German reunification. I am certain I said, "we're living big history, good bet Germany reunites." After these shards and threads, the main event fades to black.

My interrupted departure for home, however, I recall in exacting, dead certain detail.

When the panel finished, I didn't stay to chat. As I left the auditorium, a woman intercepted me in the hallway and planted herself directly in front of me. She wore hippie regalia, circa 1968, bandana in frizzed hair, faded jeans, and a dyed pearl-button shirt slashed by acid patterns. The crow's feet pinching her eyes said high side of forty.

She smiled a crooked smile, then raised a long index finger and unloaded with smug glee, "You write books about war, right? With the end of the Cold War and so many people waging peace, I guess you'll have to find another subject, eh?"

In her scolding universe, I was clearly a rough beast. This thought flashed through my mind: *Korea—that unfinished Cold War could explode as we speak.* But with two kids at home, I didn't have six hours to catalog the wars haunting her dawning age of bliss. I kept my reply civil, sincere, and accurate, "Well, ma'am, it's quite a hazardous form of peace."

Her lips pursed.

Circling the confrontational peace wager, I headed for the exit and the parking lot.

* * * * *

Cold War warriors in the West welcomed with relief and excited anticipation the Berlin Wall's demise and what it signaled. Soviet soldiers and East German police did not respond by machine gunning East and West Germans celebrating in the streets. The silent automatic weapons—the Kremlin's decision to refrain from using its military element of power to coercively repress Eastern Europe—confirmed a major change in Soviet policy was underway.

Russian Diplomatic, ideological (Information), Military, and Economic power—DIME, the acronym for the elements of power—had diminished. (See chapter one for more on DIME.) The Cold

War's long economic and political siege had weakened the Soviet empire to the point Kremlin leaders could no longer deny its decay.

Yet the Cold War had only begun to end. Winding down a sustained clash between powerful human organizations, much less a multi-decade struggle between nuclear-armed political giants, is a rocky, surprise-ridden process. The Kremlin's decision to refrain from machine-gunning East Germans, Poles, Balts, and Russians did make "the big one"—a thermonuclear war between the Soviet Union and the US—very unlikely. However, doubts galore stalked this less belligerent Russian "policy cocktail" of political and economic retrenchment. Though February 1990 held great promise, freedom-seeking citizens in Eastern Europe's collapsing Communist dictatorships faced precarious circumstances. In December 1989, vengeful subordinates assassinated Romanian dictator Nicolae Ceauşescu. Fortunately, the tyrannicide did not ignite a civil war, but when a tyrant falls, violence stalks the resulting domestic power vacuum.

The rule of thumb that power abhors a vacuum also applies in international affairs. The hallway peace wager apparently expected an era of utopian peace would replace the Cold War. Russian frailty actually created a strategic power vacuum that guaranteed political instability from East Berlin to Vladivostok and would rattle, if not topple, Soviet client states globally. In volatile conditions like these, cagey aggressors, oppressed insurgents, ideological radicals, the ruthless, the vindictive, the ambitious, and the criminal greedy see opportunity. As imperial power ebbs they have greater freedom to act, and when they do, new armed conflicts can erupt abruptly and dormant wars may reignite.

The cagey and oppressed definitely seized the moment. Here are some examples: within six months of February 1990, Iraqi dictator

Saddam Hussein invaded Kuwait and ignited a major war in the Middle East; within sixteen months, Yugoslavia fragmented into a nest of small wars and genocidal slaughter; and within two years, the Soviet Union itself fragmented (December 1991).

After the August 1991 coup d'etat against Soviet leader Mikhail Gorbachev failed, the USSR dissolved with comparatively minimal violence. Its "soviet socialist republics" became independent states, more or less. However, other would-be nation states failed to escape Moscow's prison. Russia did not recognize the Chechnya region's declaration of independence. In 1994, Russian military forces invaded and a bloodletting ensued.

The first three example conflicts involved nation states directly or indirectly influenced by the ebb of Soviet power. China's aggressive territorial expansion in the South China Sea pre-dated the USSR's collapse. In 1974, China forcibly seized an island claimed by South Vietnam. In 1979, China and Vietnam (reunified by victorious North Vietnam) fought a bitter border war (see chapter three). The Soviet Union did not intervene, but it backed Hanoi in that fight and remained a firm Vietnamese military ally. China and Vietnam clashed in the Spratly Islands in 1988. By 1990, Russia's evident weakness had reduced the Kremlin's ability to provide its allies and client states with military aid and diplomatic support—especially ones confronting the People's Republic of China. I suspect cagey Beijing concluded it had even greater freedom of action in Southeast Asia, for its southern maritime adventures accelerate post-1990. In early 1992, China illegally deployed combat troops on a South China Sea island claimed by Vietnam, Da Luc Reef (in the Paracel Islands). With this act of post-1990 war-making, Beijing seized the contested territory and did so with very little diplomatic retaliation or media attention and no economic penalty. Western diplomats and media were focused on turbulent Russia, the Middle East, and the 1992 US presidential election.

Hutu and Tutsi ethnic antipathy in central Africa definitely pre-dates the Cold War. Hutu-Tutsi on-off ethnic bloodlettings in central and eastern Africa have minimal, if not nil, connection to Eurasian power struggles. Ethnic warfare, however, can be as deadly as war waged by nation states. During the 1994 Rwandan genocide, Hutu ethnic extremists massacred over eight hundred thousand innocents. Then the Rwandan Hutu-Tutsi war spread to eastern Congo with murderous effects that would not begin to subside until 2003 (see chapter six).

My reply to the hallway peace wager, "Quite a hazardous form of peace," was much too optimistic. The five selected examples of organized group violence that occurred within approximately fifty months of February 1990 either seeded, spurred, perpetuated, or expanded roughly three dozen serious wars—each war a wicked cocktail from hell.

Critical Concept: Wicked Problems

Wicked. A genocide is wicked, in the common definition of evil. There is, however, a class of problems called "wicked problems." While wicked problems are not necessarily evil, they do test human intellect and trounce human arrogance. Warfare is definitely a wicked problem: a problem with a multitude of interdependent variables—a dynamic death-dealing power cocktail shaped by calculation, incompetence, and chance—that is exceedingly difficult, if not impossible to resolve. Because a wicked problem constantly evolves (it is dynamic and never static), the wicked problem now is never quite the same wicked problem it was. Wicked problem data are always incomplete and often contradictory. "Known unknown" data and "unknown unknown" data issues vex wicked problems. Bits and pieces of a wicked problem—known variables—can be identified. However, interdependence between and among variables is difficult to determine and their degree of interdependency is often uncertain. The act of solving one "sub-problem" variable or even attempting to solve it may exacerbate another component problem or create a new problem variable—a self-inflicted total surprise.

Framing or defining a problem is a key conceptual step in problem solving. Once a problem is "framed," the would-be problem solver can better determine the resources required to address it and then develop a plan to apply those resources with the goal of solving it.

However, a wicked problem resists analytic framing. Iffy data, hazy variable interdependence, and unpredictable change mean a wicked problem behaves something like an unbounded energy field that defies the laws of physics. No equation confines it. To employ another metaphor, wicked problem investigators can identify colors, detect brush strokes, see paint squirt in real time, and spot calculation and design in the cocktail swirl, but no mental or digital canvas can quite capture a wicked problem for definitive analysis.

Testing intellect, trouncing arrogance, a wicked problem resists solution, much less a satisfactory real-world political conclusion. What a mess.

Yet some wicked problems must be engaged by the responsible among us, for they are life-or-death matters. You may not want war, you may reject its slaughter and waste, but at an inconvenient point in your time on Earth, the wicked and violent interactive group-process problem of war may ignore your wishes—and want you.

* * * * *

Whether a mixed drink or geo-strategic policy, a cocktail is a combination.

A superb Manhattan combines these ingredients: sweet vermouth, rye, dash of orange bitters, ice, a Luxardo cherry, and an orange peel slice. Drink up.

In a professional prize fight, professional boxers avoid wild blows in favor of tactical combinations that mix maneuver and punches—bob, weave to gain position, feint a right jab, then throw a knockout left uppercut. The best fighters and their trainers spend hours in the gym perfecting these combinations.

A professional championship bout is a controlled competition governed by rules set by the sanctioning boxing association. The referee in the ring enforces the rules.

But what happens when the ref is bribed? Instead of serving as an honest arbiter, a bribed ref becomes a saboteur, a criminal. No longer sport, the bout is a sham rigged by mobsters.

In war, however, bribery may be a legitimate weapon, a means of exerting power or enhancing another means of exerting power. A fighter-bomber preparing to launch weapons while receiving real-time targeting intelligence from on-the-ground commandos is participating in a military operation that consists of several integrated "pieces" (sub-operations)—a dynamic cocktail, if you think of the weapons, personnel, and communications gear as very sophisticated ingredients. A narrative crafted to stir angry passions in a restive populace can be the most potent weapon in a plot to trigger rebellion. The explosive narrative, however, needs a delivery system, so the insurgents pay sleazy media types to repeat it, relentlessly and uncritically. Since bribery fuels the human narrative delivery systems, it is a critical ingredient in the rebels' political cocktail.

The Roman historian Sallust tells us in the last two decades of the second century BC, Berber rebel Jugurtha used bribery, murder, and insurgent raids to build a personal power base in Numidia (modern-day Algeria). The cunning Jugurtha repeatedly thwarted Roman army efforts to catch and defeat him. With its legions bogged down in a no-win North African sand trap, Roman authorities co-opted Jugurtha's father-in-law and ally, Bocchus. They bribed Bocchus by promising him territory. The palm-greased father-in-law sent Jugurtha to Rome in chains.

Bribery secured Rome's strategic goal, so it served as an effective weapon. The legions, however, contributed to the Roman warfighting cocktail. Their armed presence gave Bocchus a sobering motive to accept Rome's deal. The operational combination of legions and bribery defeated Jugurtha's insurgency. Rome's cocktail mixed military (its army's kinetic threat) and non-military (diplomatic, psychological, non-kinetic intimidation) operations. Roman combination warfare ended the wicked Jugurthine War.

Critical Concept: Warfare Without Limits

The book *Unrestricted Warfare* (also known as *Warfare Without Limits*) is a serious thought experiment that should be subtitled *How to Make Cocktails from Hell to Defeat China's Enemies.* Authored by People's Liberation Army Air Force colonels Qiao Liang and Wang Xiangsui (Qiao is now a major general) and published by the PLA Literature and Arts Publishing House in 1999, the book contemplates the ways and means and reasons twenty-first-century political actors might prepare and serve deadly policy combinations to their adversaries.

In their afterword, the authors identify their book's origin: the 1996 near "showdown" in the Taiwan Strait (Qiao and Wang 1999, 253–254). China indicated it might attack Taiwan. Two US Navy aircraft-carrier battle groups intervened. "People were suddenly moved to 'think up strategies when facing a situation,'"—the situation being a naval battle between China and the US, if not a major war that could involve nuclear weapons.

This revelation opens an important window on their thought experiment. Qiao and Wang were senior officers serving a rising power that might as well clash again with the United States. I emphasize the phrase "clash again." In November 1950, the Korean War became a US–China war; in many respects it remained so in 1999. As this book is written, American–Chinese competition and cooperation on the Korean peninsula remains critical to the Korean War's resolution, whether by diplomacy or combat.

The colonels, as Chinese strategists, had the duty to peer ahead, speculate on future geo-strategic conditions, and mull ways and means to defeat America in those conditions. Their American adversaries have reciprocated. In late 1992, I was serving as a strategic war gaming consultant in the Secretary of Defense's Office of Net Assessments. Net Assessments director, the great Andrew Marshall, presented his consultants with a long-term thought experiment, one to ponder on and off the payroll. How could the US fight and win a war for national survival against China circa 2020 or 2025? Consider the political, technological, economic, military, social, bilateral, regional, and global contexts. Then repeat the thought experiment again and again.

* * * * *

In their conclusion, Qiao and Wang observe:

"War is the most difficult to explain and understand. It needs support from technology, but technology cannot substitute for morale and stratagem; it needs artistic inspiration, but rejects romanticism and sentimentalism; it needs mathematical precision, but precision can sometimes render it mechanical and rigid; it needs philosophical abstraction, but pure thinking does not help to seize short-lived opportunities amid iron and fire."

War is difficult to explain, difficult to understand, and, like the future, tough to predict. The unexpected and unforeseen occur; unknown unknowns—missing data and knowledge the planners and strategists do not even know exist—flummox "mechanical" responses and confound linear thinkers. Pondering variables and variable possibilities in advance might give creative leaders an edge in detecting and seizing emerging opportunities in "iron and fire" (chaotic) circumstances.

Critical Concepts: Wicked Dynamics

Chapter one in *Cocktails from Hell* attempts to do several things. It defines for readers essential terms such as "tactical," "operational," and "strategic." Instead of mulling policy cocktails that might disrupt or defeat the United States, the chapter suggests that Qiao and Wang's various examples of tactical and operational troublemaking and a version of their multi-domain "cocktail analysis" are useful tools for helping readers assess the wicked dynamics of current and future conflicts. Official Washington now has a bureaucratic name for these cocktails of power: coordinated coercive diplomacy. Coordinated is the ideal condition, for their real-world execution is often slapdash. When one belligerent's cocktail mixes with an adversary's concoction, a truly wicked war is the typical result—in this book's anti-bureaucrat lingo, a cocktail from hell.

In each conflict chapter (chapters two–six) I attempt to use these tools to address the following questions:

- What energizes the conflict?
- Who are the key actors, what do they want that brings them into the war, and how do they contribute to the conflict's wicked dynamics?
- What benefits do the actors think their efforts will obtain?

Each chapter sketches some (by no means all) of the historical events and issues that shape the current conflict. This approach treats conflict origins as a dynamic process and is often more helpful than attempting to identify a specific "source" or "cause" of a war. Every chapter has sub-sections summarizing participant (actor) capabilities, interests, and goals. Each chapter includes illustrative participant policies and operations and, in some cases, how war's wicked dynamics have altered them. Every chapter includes at least one hypothetical operation or alternative course of action a participant might consider. Occasionally a sub-section will highlight the key "cocktail ingredients" involved in a particular policy or operation—the key elements of power utilized, the relevant means of exerting power, or an important context to consider (see chapter one).

The "Conflict Scenarios" section in each chapter sketches possible futures—I repeat, *possible*. The scenarios are illustrative projections, not predictions. The scenarios were created utilizing historical and war gaming analytic techniques that James F. Dunnigan and I employed in all four editions of *A Quick and Dirty Guide to War* (1985, 1992, 1996, and 2008).

The five wars examined in this book are deadly realities in various stages of ignition, explosion, transformation, or remission. However, the issues and problems energizing these wicked problems will confront senior political leaders throughout the remainder of the century. Variations on the techniques, tactics, and operational "power" cocktails employed by participants in these conflicts will challenge—and possibly threaten—warfighters and peace wagers worldwide. Analyzing these "shaping" wars as processes benefits future leaders and informed citizens.

Chapter Two: The Korean War, as I thought in 1990 when accosted by the peace wager, "could explode as we speak." It could also conclude with a negotiated settlement. However, other "frozen wars" and "wars of nuclear proliferation" vex the planet, so the twenty-first-century Korean War is a laboratory. Whatever the outcome, the Korean War diplomacy of 2017–2018 has been fascinating and the chapter includes a "first brush" sub-section examining the Trump administration's diplomatic "policy cocktail" implemented with the goal of denuclearizing North Korea.

Chapter Three: China's muscular economic, military, and diplomatic-information ventures in the South China Sea and the Himalayas are already shaping the century. Call it imperialism with twenty-first-century Chinese characteristics.

Chapter Four: Russia's revived "czarist" empire has snagged in Ukraine. Even a risk-taking nuclear power needs cash to modernize twenty-first-century conventional forces.

Chapter Five: In pursuit of grandiose imperial dreams, Iran's clerical dictatorship wages chaotic war in Yemen. Yemen pits Shia Muslim Iran against Sunni Muslim Saudi Arabia. Starvation is a weapon of mass destruction in Yemen's tribal/ethnic/sectarian conflagration.

Chapter Six: Congo, the land of armed peacekeeping, crime, feudalism, ethnic wars, and very valuable mineral deposits.

No matter tomorrow's news—surrender, shooting war, negotiated deal, revolution, disintegration—each conflict offers insights for waging war and waging peace in the next five to eight decades.

—AUSTIN BAY

Austin, Texas and Wharton, Texas, September 2017–March 2018

CHAPTER 1

COCKTAIL CONCEPTS, POLITICAL WARFARE, AMBITION, AND AVARICE

According to Qiao and Wang, war is difficult "to explain and understand" and defining "war" with any precision is difficult.

So the colonels, like other soldiers and scholars, have a spacious definition of war.

Spacious—or flexible—is real-world smart. In spring 2018, academic and media sources estimated that from eighty to one hundred fifty wars were savaging the world. Other commentators (I among them) argued for higher totals.

Addressing the question "How many wars are occurring in the Democratic Republic of Congo (DRC)?" bares the statistical iffyness. A defensible estimate is "maybe twenty." To reply "forty or so" isn't hyperbolic. Between 1996 and 2003, three to five million people died in the grisly cocktail from hell now called the Great Congo War. At least a dozen smaller wars contributed to that tragic conflagration, including the 1994 Rwandan genocide mentioned in the introduction.

Most thoughtful definitions frame warfare as a type of collective human effort. The *Oxford English Dictionary* defines war as "any active hostility or struggle between living beings; a conflict between opposing forces or principles." That definition excludes the introduction's boxing match, for the bout's hostility is promotional, not blood fatal. The loser gets a paycheck. The dictionary definition could include a duel—"two combatants" is plural. (The battle between David and Goliath is a biblical example of champion warfare where two heroes fight to settle a tribal or community dispute.) A common sense interpretation suffices: warfare requires collective effort. "Struggle" indicates that war involves a degree of sustained effort. Waging sustained war takes a group of human beings. Since human beings in a group use intragroup politics to organize their group and reach decisions, it follows that waging war is a type of political endeavor (a point Carl von Clausewitz made). When a discrete group (ethnic group, clan, sectarian group, political organization, gang, village collective, family) actively fights another discrete group for some purpose for a sustained period of time, that rates as war. The "maybe twenty" estimate for the number of current wars in the DRC meets that basic definition. For Pygmies (Batwa tribe) in the Katanga and Tanganyika provinces, their struggle with the Bantu Luba people is a war for survival. The community-identity marker of ethnicity matters in this war. So does the economic context. The Pygmies are predominantly hunter-gatherers. The Bantus are farmers. Land use rights—hunt or farm?—is a central issue. The Pygmies contend that their clashes with the Katangan separatist Bakata-Katanga militia entwines with their struggle with the Luba. However, the Bakata-Katanga militia also battles other Katangan tribes, the provincial government, and the national government.

Two wars in Katanga Province? Or more? (For more on Congolese ethnic warfare, see chapter six.)

* * * * *

Violent physical (kinetic) interaction between and among human beings runs from a bloodless shoving match (perhaps warlike, but not war) to a full-spectrum, high-intensity war for national survival fought by belligerent "Great Powers" using nuclear and genetically-engineered biological weapons.

Yet conflict without bullets can kill. Non-kinetic means methods such as financial warfare and sanctions warfare, which can cripple enemy economies and possibly starve people en masse. When do non-kinetic measures—for example, relentless cyber attacks on financial institutions and electricity distribution grids—so weaken and disrupt an adversary that they become acts of war? Informed answers differ.

Violence is a form of communication, but what level of violent, kinetic interaction rises to warfare? Informed answers to this question also differ.

Intelligence analysts and experienced military planners tend to agree that a gray zone separates street-gang battles in Los Angeles and the episodic, low-intensity civil war fought in the streets of Bangui, the capital of the Central African Republic (CAR). Most experts will sensibly argue that the vastly dissimilar political, cultural, economic, and infrastructure contexts between Los Angeles and Bangui are determinative; the LA street action classifies as violent crime and Bangui's torment as anarchic war. However, LA cops and UN peacekeeping troops note that the LA gangs and the

3

sectarian CAR militias battling for control of a Bangui neighborhood use similar tactics. Both gang thugs and militiamen arm themselves with knives and Molotov cocktails and sometimes AK-47-type rifles. For cops and soldiers in a crossfire, the tactical gray zone between high-intensity criminal violence and low-intensity war shrinks to a meaningless sliver.

* * * * *

Congo's deadly tragedy combines calculated design, hideous violence, desire, and chaos that usually mixes crime and war. Qiao and Wang's techniques help make sense of this wicked mix. In chapter two of *Warfare Without Limits* (a section subtitled "What Means and Methods Are Used to Fight?"), Qiao and Wang list numerous means, methods, and techniques for waging warfare that they argue will add toxicity to twenty-first century combination warfare—cocktails they might help blend and serve on behalf of the People's Republic of China.

The cocktail concept has deep roots. In chapter five of his treatise *The Art of War*, the great Chinese strategist Sun Tzu argued that "combat power in battle" was an "exercise of regular and irregular actions; variations in irregular and regular actions can never be limited." They "perpetually engender each other like a ring without a breach." (Huang 2009, 58).

Given their employer, it's no surprise that the PLAAF officers' means and schemes list reflects Mao Tse-Tung's dictum that "politics is war without bloodshed, while war is politics with bloodshed." Chairman Mao used conceptually similar cocktails to sow mayhem long before the last decade of the twentieth century. Other strategists and academic institutions have published comparable lists of political warfare gambits.

Here's a partial list from their tome; in some cases, the colonels' brief description of the method or technique is included.

- Psychological warfare ("spreading rumors to intimidate the enemy and break down his will")
- Smuggling warfare ("throwing markets into confusion and attacking economic order")
- Media warfare ("manipulating what people see and hear in order to lead public opinion along")
- Drug warfare ("obtaining sudden and huge illicit profits by spreading disaster in other countries")
- Technological warfare ("creating monopolies by setting standards independently")
- Fabrication warfare ("presenting a counterfeit appearance of real strength before the eyes of the enemy"—deception)
- Resources warfare ("plundering stores of resources")
- Economic aid warfare ("bestowing favor in the open and contriving to control matters in secret")
- Cultural warfare ("leading cultural trends along in order to assimilate those with different views")
- International law warfare ("seizing the earliest opportunity to set up regulations")
- Precision warfare ("characterized by concealment, speed, accuracy, a high degree of effectiveness, and few collateral casualties")
- Trade warfare

- Financial warfare
- Traditional terror warfare ("bombings, kidnappings, assassinations, and plane hijackings")
- New terror warfare ("the rendezvous of terrorists with various types of new high technologies that possibly will evolve into new super weapons")
- Ecological warfare (modern technology influencing "the natural state of rivers, oceans, the crust of the earth, the polar ice sheets, the air circulating in the atmosphere, and the ozone layer"—may be quasi-theoretical)

I think nuclear proliferation warfare should be on the list—perhaps it is, as a not-so-new super weapon within new terror. Their book is a thought experiment, so their list and categories are indicative, not comprehensive. Cyber warfare doesn't appear on this particular list; however, cyber communication technology and cyber warfare permeate the book. Qiao and Wang were savvy. Every piece of digital communication—email, social media post, phone, text—can be captured, stored, and retrieved.

The colonels' sketches of psychological and media warfare overlap with a buzz term that American national security agencies and commentators have begun using: narrative warfare. The term has explanatory value. Narrative warfare employs "weaponized narratives" spun from "highly selective truth[s]," outright lies, false accusations, distorted and altered quotations, emotional appeals, sensational outrage, fear mongering, blame shifting, intimidating threats, victim posturing, virtue signaling, and fabricated imagery. Indeed, these disruptive and often destructive techniques—with the possible exception of fabricated imagery—have been in the human political and psychological warfare tool kit since the human species arose. However, modern mass media and digital communications can quickly and pervasively spread the weaponized narrative, often without challenge.

Advocates for the distinctiveness of narrative warfare insist that this narrative and technology cocktail can create a powerful psychological weapon capable of quickly influencing national and international opinion. Cagey warfighters will dynamically link weaponized narratives to other kinetic and non-kinetic operations in an ongoing conflict and create a powerful operational cocktail. For example, narrative warfare linked to a false flag operation may shape or alter an election. Criminal speculators could use the same combination to destroy an honest company's reputation, sell the company's stock short, then spread the "big lie" to drive the stock price down.

The weaponized narrative's combination of speed and pervasiveness can create psychological vulnerabilities in an adversary's population. In a long war or extended diplomatic confrontation, fear and doubt seeded by an adversary's weaponized narratives may erode its opponent's will to continue to struggle.

Some analysts argue that democracies are more vulnerable to weaponized narrative attacks than authoritarian states that strictly control or deny freedom of speech and freedom of the press.

Nations have always used narratives to support their diplomatic operations. Not all of them are weaponized, but a powerful, moving story gives a diplomatic initiative additional energy. Often these narratives incorporate national or ethnic historical and cultural themes. Since they support a diplomatic initiative, they are always political.

Qiao and Wang's selected war-making ingredients and ingredient categories and the handful I added are tools for understanding the wicked dynamics stirring a cocktail from hell. Psychological warfare, smuggling warfare, economic aid warfare, and resources warfare, in various combinations in various locales, plague Congo. The cultural warfare in the Kasai region is intense. "Rumor warfare" in Kasai is not a discrete war, but rumors have intensified the conflict. In eastern Congo, the smuggling wars complicate the battles waged by local militias, government forces, and UN peacekeepers. The combinations in Kasai and eastern Congo are truly wicked.

The Four Levels of War

Contemporary military analysts typically identify four levels of war; from low to high division they are: (1) the Tactical Level (tactics and basic combat action, such as an infantry squad on a battlefield), (2) the Operational Level, (3) the Strategic Level, and (4) Grand Strategy.

Qiao and Wang use the terms "battles" (tactical military combat), "campaigns-operational art" (operational), "war-strategy" (strategic), and "war policy" ("grand war" or grand strategy).

These categories are squishy collectives; in the real world, they are a spectrum of activities. Tactical combat can and does have strategic effects. A classic assassination conducted by a single agent is usually a tactical action, but assassinating an Austrian grand duke in 1914 Bosnia helped spark World War One's strategic holocaust. The operational level focuses on campaigns. Though the term has flexibility, a campaign usually consists of preparing for and fighting a linked series of battles. Grant's Vicksburg campaign is regarded as an instructive example of linking battles (fighting a series of battles) to secure a specific objective that attained strategic economic and political goals (Union control of the Mississippi River and splitting the South). Strategy addresses military and non-military actions and objectives at the national level: in other words, the level where the belligerent's internal group politics and economic and demographic wherewithal to provide war material and personnel are major considerations. Grand strategy considers longer-term national and international military and non-military contexts and actions in warfare.

Philip II, Alexander the Great's father, created the first genuine tactical combined-arms army. Philip armed the Macedonian armored infantry phalanx with a longer spear. He trained his outstanding cavalry to operate as a strike unit that used the phalanx as a "fixing" force. To connect the slow but powerful phalanx and the mobile horsemen, he formed a lightly armored infantry corps of soldier-athletes, the hypaspists. Here is a "tactical presentation" of the Macedonian combined-arms army advancing toward an enemy: As the slow, formidable phalanx moved forward and the quick cavalry probed the enemy line and flank for vulnerabilities, the hypaspists moved like a hinge, protecting the phalanx's flank while maintaining contact with the horsemen. The mobile hypaspists provided an armed battlefield communications link between the cavalry and the slow-moving phalanx. With Alexander in command—and leadership is a cocktail ingredient—this flexible and lethal tactical military cocktail won victories from Anatolia to Egypt to Mesopotamia to India.

To defeat Persia, Alexander had to militarily and politically secure the eastern Mediterranean littoral. Taking the cities of Sidon and Tyre protected his army's strategic rear. With the strategic battlefield prepared, Alexander turned east to attack the Persian Empire's heartland.

China's 1950 invasion of Tibet seized the Himalayan high ground. In the 1962 Sino-Indian War, China took control of the key passes leading south into India (see chapter three).

Alexander's victory at Gaugamela (331 BC) wowed Qiao and Wang and they said so in their thought experiment. According to the colonels, in that decisive battle, Alexander demonstrated the "ability to use the flexibility of the cavalry and the stability of the foot soldiers" to achieve "the ideal combination" to defeat the Persian (Iranian) army under Darius III. Quite a tactical combination. I interpret "stability" to indicate the phalanx's fixing-force role—the Macedonian phalanx was deadly and could not be ignored. A fixing force of some type (not necessarily military) plays a role in the wars this book examines. According to Arrian, prior to the battle of Gaugamela, Alexander rejected a recommendation that he launch a night attack and catch the Persians unprepared. The Macedonian, however, thought a surprise night attack might give Darius an excuse for Persian defeat. Alexander would not steal a victory; he would conquer in open daylight and "without artifice." The Great's cocktails included narrative warfare as combined-arms tactics.

Qiao and Wang, however, claim China fielded the first combined-arms army. According to the colonels, in the eleventh century BC (probably 1046 BC), King Wu of the Zhou Dynasty used a combined-arms army of a sort to defeat King Zhuo of the Shang Dynasty. King Wu's force had armored infantry, warriors (probably light infantry), and vehicles (chariots).

The colonels agree that Wu and Alexander were military cocktail warfare masters supreme.

From chapter five of their book:

"King Wu of the Zhou Dynasty three thousand years ago and Alexander the Great over two thousand years ago definitely would not have known what a cocktail was, and yet they were both masters of mixing 'cocktails' on the battlefield. This is because, like mixing a cocktail, they were adept at ingeniously combining two or more battlefield factors together, throwing them into battle, and gaining victories."

Cocktail Political Warfare

For decades, US military war colleges have emphasized operationally and strategically combining and coordinating the elements of power to gain advantage at the operational and strategic levels— create a dynamic, synergistic power cocktail to gain advantage in the political action known as war.

The elements of power are most simply expressed by the acronym DIME: diplomacy, information, military, and economic. They are ways to express and apply power. Information was once called "psychological," a term Qiao and Wang use in a narrower sense. Sometimes "I" stood for intelligence, which is a type of information, unless you consider all information to be intelligence of a type (and some sharp soldiers do). Narrative warfare and media operations would be considered subsets of "I"—information/intelligence.

If this seems a bit confusing, no worries, once again the indicative counts. Boundaries in real-world human activity are relative. Beyond the classroom, the elements of power are not always discrete. Cleanly separating diplomatic and economic operations is often difficult; the US post-WWII Marshall Plan was a diplo-econ-security hybrid supported by relentless reminders (information/advertising) that a prosperous "free world" was a vital American objective.

British strategist Colin Gray describes several contexts for waging a war: political, social-cultural, economic, military-strategic, technological, geographical, and historical. Some strategists argue his social-cultural and military-strategic contexts are conflated. Don't sweat the academic skirmishing. Gray's contexts for waging a war serve as additional guidance for assessing cocktails from hell. Geography matters—ask Ukraine, Vietnam, and both Koreas about geographic proximity to a Great Power or an emerging Great Power. (See chapter two's discussion of the Korean peninsula's betweenness.)

Military and intelligence/information operations are executed on the land, on and under the sea, in the air, in space, and in cyber space. These "regions," as some commentators call them, constitute a geography of a type. To distinguish them from geographic regions, military analysts now tend to use the buzzword "domain" to describe them.

DIME, however, served as excellent guidance for planners and leaders—a doctrine of sorts for assessing options and then executing the operations in the world. DIME as an acronym, however, short-changed planners seeking a quick reference guide to the questions "What else can we do?"; "What else matters?"; and "What other options should we consider when trying to develop multi-dimensional policies and fight complex wars?" American jargonologists expanded DIME to DIMEFILCH, including FILCH: financial, intelligence, legal (law enforcement), cultural, and humanitarian capabilities. Different DIMEFILCH combinations produce different policy cocktails. The word "humanitarian" sounds positive and, in diplo-speak, it usually is. However, effects matter. A cocktail warrior might argue a huge refugee surge, whatever the cause, is a "humanitarian attack" that presents his adversary with messy economic, military, cultural, information, and legal issues. Guess what—it does. China fears such a surge from a collapsed North Korea.

America's military war colleges always stress coordination. Amid Qiao's and Wang's "iron and fire"—in the midst of a violent crisis—diplomats, soldiers, logisticians, and planners tasked with war fighting might find a simple implementation/coordination acronym handy. Organization matters in implementation. An organization requires coordinating leadership, so leadership is a critical element in the effective use of power. Change happens—which is a cool way of putting it—so the policy cocktail must be dynamic, not static. As wicked problems evolve, flexibility (adaptability) in execution becomes an advantage. Adapting while engaged in the wicked process requires insight, judgment, and decision—all three involve leadership and organization. Maintaining sufficient resources and identifying new resources are both essential actions—resources tangible and intangible. Sustained morale matters a great deal in executing policy, so whether we call it morale, will, or resolve, that semi-tangible resource is so fundamental to the effective and sustained use of power that it deserves elite acknowledgment. Besides, Clausewitz defined war as a clash of wills. Will, adaptability, resources, organization, leadership? WAROL? Too militant for diplomats waging peace or do you see Andy Warhol's Campbell's soup can? Substitute flexibility for adaptability and presto, FLOWR. FLOWR power 2028, not 1968.

The five wars this book examines feature integrated, multidimensional warfare using kinetic and non-kinetic means. We can see the outlines of multidimensional political cocktail warfare and sometimes detect the skeletons. The North Korean regime's key political policy, shock lethality, combines military kinetic action (violence) with information action using methods Qiao and Wang might call psychological and media warfare. Shock lethality also has elements of new terror war. China, Russia, and Iran have their own methods and doctrinal terms for organizing and conducting political warfare.

MONUSCO, the UN peacekeeping operation in Congo, has conducted combined DIMEFILCH efforts at the operational and strategic levels. The Trump administration's maximum-pressure policy to de-nuclearize North Korea leveraged DIMEFILCH combinations tactically, operationally, and strategically.

* * * * *

Cocktails from hell, however, are not bureaucratic or academic exercises in statecraft. They are dangerous, violent actions and reactions of deed and word, in which people risk death and people are killed and maimed and psychologically scarred. These monsters beggar economies. That means passions and emotions mix in these cocktails.

On the land, in the air, on and under the sea, in orbit, people will risk death and kill for concrete reasons, such as access to resources or to defend their homes—or to defend their cyber space. The "what if" is obvious. If the home defender's territory has resources that the resource accessor needs or desires, access to resources and defense of home can (and often do) lead to bloodletting. This cocktail is mixing in the South China Sea.

Passions and emotions are fundamental elements of human behavior—what the wise among us call "the human condition." The

Italian poet Petrarch acknowledged that dark desires and emotions frustrate peacemaking when he wrote "Five great enemies to peace inhabit within us: avarice, ambition, envy, anger, and pride. If those enemies were to be banished we should infallibly enjoy perpetual peace." Petrarch listed the essentials. All five of these great enemies, when expressed in real-world physical action, can threaten other human beings. Fear and hate are both emotions that are aroused or provoked by perceived threat.

Intellects confined by behavioral science might dismiss Petrarch's Renaissance enemies list unless the adjective "sociopathic" modifies each trait. "Sociopathic" definitely describes our species' worst monsters; when a sociopath wields political authority within a group, the chance of violent excess magnifies. Pathology, however, is actually a reductionist explanation for the wicked, interactive, group process of warfare. Few among us are clinical sociopaths; Petrarch's great enemies inhabit every human being. The history of balance-of-power politics—the Cold War's nuclear mutual assured destruction (MAD), for example—and of power vacuums (see introduction) suggests that adjectives such as "unchecked," "unappeasable," "unpunished," "benighted," or even "pigheaded" better describe most war-generating circumstances. Pigheaded avarice, ambition, envy, anger, and pride expressed in policy decisions and operational cocktails certainly prolong wars and also start them.

CHAPTER 2

NORTH KOREA

Frozen War, Hot Nukes, Maximum Pressure Cocktails

For six decades, two problems from hell have haunted American leaders and Washington foreign policy whiz kids: ending the Korean War and halting nuclear proliferation. On the Korean peninsula, the problems combine in a century-shaping cocktail from hell. As this book was written, on-going events simultaneously suggested two rather contradictory outcomes: (1) North Korean nuclear attacks on South Korean, Japanese, and American mega-cities in the Pacific basin that resulted in a radioactive North Korea and a globally impoverishing East Asian regional war; and (2) a Korean War peace treaty made possible by a very peculiar deal. The very peculiar deal—North Korea's young, flabby, and utterly criminal dictator exchanging his regime's nuclear weapons for American, South Korean, Japanese, and Chinese investment—and promises he

Chapter Abbreviation Key

ABM = Anti-ballistic missile
CVID = Complete, Verifiable, Irreversible De-nuclearization
DPRK = Democratic People's Republic of Korea (North Korea)
DMZ = De-militarized zone
ICBM = Intercontinental ballistic missile
IRBM = Intermediate range ballistic missile
PRC = People's Republic of China
ROK = Republic of Korea (South Korea)
SRBM = Short-range ballistic missile
THAAD = Terminal high-altitude area defense, a U.S. Army medium-range anti-missile missile. The USN's SM-3 (deployed on Aegis ships) has a longer range.
UAV = Unmanned aerial vehicle (drone)

will live to enjoy his nation's economic success and South Korean K-pop girl bands rocking Pyongyang.

Overview

The Korean War never really ended. The war is (was?) a "frozen conflict" that began in the Cold War era. However, time didn't freeze, the actors didn't freeze, and the conflict slowly metastasized as North Korea's belligerent dictatorship acquired nuclear weapons and long-range delivery capabilities.

As the twenty-first century's second decade concludes, a truncated but dangerous version of the twentieth century's Cold War persists on the Korean peninsula, complete with the ideological facet of Communist (North Korea) versus the free world (South Korea). The antagonists' large conventional armies confront one another from fortified positions along the DMZ that the July 1953 armistice created. The armistice is not a peace treaty but a ceasefire agreement halting the slugfest conventional war that began in June 1950, when North Korean forces launched a surprise invasion of South Korea.

Conventional combat never totally ceased. Since 1953, Pyongyang has repeatedly shattered the ceasefire, waging belligerent fits in a calculated, contained, yet always deadly war of aggression against South Korea (see the following discussion of the DMZ Conflict). The March 26, 2010 attack on the corvette *Cheonan* is a particularly bloody example. Forty-six ROK sailors died when a North Korean torpedo sank the ship; it was the highest death toll from a single North Korean attack since the 1960s. The North Korean dictatorship's grievous ceasefire violations document in spilled blood a key political policy of the regime: shock lethality. (DPRK shock lethality operations have military, information, narrative, diplomatic, and regime maintenance goals.)

* * * * *

In the early 1990s, as the Cold War faded on other fronts, the Korean War's nuclear proliferation battle began to escalate. Under the leadership of Kim Il Sung (Kim 1, the man who led the 1950 invasion of South Korea), the DPRK expanded a nascent nuclear weapons program. When Kim 1 died in 1994, his son Kim Jong Il (Kim 2) replaced him and the regime became a hereditary Communist dictatorship. Kim Jong Il and his son and successor, Kim Jong Un (Kim 3), have continued the nuclear quest, violating non-proliferation agreements and evading international weapons proliferation sanctions. Kim 2 and Kim 3 continued to intensively pursue the regime's unique brand of economic diplomacy: criminal sovereignty.

The Kim regime's successful acquisition of nuclear weapons and delivery systems became the preeminent issue in Korea's unfinished war. Moreover, the regime relentlessly threatened to launch nuclear attacks against South Korea and its allies, Japan and the US.

Nuclear weapons ended World War II, the first nuclear war. If diplomacy falters, nuclear detonations still might end the Korean War.

Key Actors, Their Goals and Risks

North Korea: The dictatorship won the nuclear proliferation war and acquired ICBMs with nuclear warheads. By some measures, the dictatorship maintains the world's fourth-largest military, though much of its equipment is obsolete.

China: Two nuclear powers, the People's Republic of China (PRC, Beijing) and Russia, share a border with North Korea. The Red Chinese Army crossed the Yalu in November 1950 and became North Korea's frontline ally. Since the end of the Cold War, the PRC has been North Korea's primary supporter.

South Korea, United States, and Japan

Diplomatic Relationships: North Korean threats have led these three nations to form an unofficial but functionally close twenty-first-century military coalition. There are internal frictions that adversaries exploit (see Known 5 in Ten Knowns, following). They are also wary of China's expanding power and Russia's still-potent military. This alliance is an economic and military powerhouse.

Strategic Military: The US is the world's most powerful nation, economically, militarily, and politically—ergo, the nickname "hyperpower." But the US isn't the whole show. South Korea (Republic of Korea, ROK) and Japan both possess modern armies, navies, and air forces that complement US capabilities. Japan's navy—the official name is Naval Self-Defense Force—possesses strategic capabilities. North Korean and Chinese threats have led Japan to revise its post-WWII constitutional restrictions on the use of military forces. Japan's public debate over its self-imposed limitations has sent a diplomatic message. When an enemy aims a nuclear warhead at Tokyo, Japanese "self-defense" may include offensive action.

The UN and United Nations Command

Strategic and Operational Diplomacy: As a diplomatic actor, the UN Security Council has repeatedly sanctioned North Korea for violating agreements and UN resolutions restricting its nuclear weapons and missile programs.

Operational Military: In North Korea's peculiar case, the UN is also a military adversary. By resolution, United Nations forces entered the war in 1950 and continue to defend South Korea. American military personnel in South Korea still ostensibly serve under the United Nations Command (UNC) in South Korea. In early 1950, the UN decided to seat the Republic of China (Taiwan) rather than Mao Tse-Tung's Communist government in Beijing. The Soviet delegation protested the decision and quit attending UN Security Council sessions. The Soviets had a point: Mao's forces had won the Chinese Civil War (see chapter six). However, the delegation's protest meant that no Soviet representative was present to veto UN Security Council Resolution 83 (July 27, 1950), which declared that North Korea had "breached the peace" and asked UN members to provide "assistance to the Republic of Korea" (South Korea). During the years of heavy combat (1950–1953), the US and South Korea supplied almost ninety percent of the military personnel serving under the UN banner. When the armistice was signed, 303,000 American and 591,000 South Korean military personnel served with the UNC. However, another fifteen nations deployed military personnel and five more (India among them) deployed civilian humanitarian aid personnel. In 1953, the UNC had large contingents of British and Australian military personnel (fourteen thousand and seventeen thousand, respectively). Canada also supplied a sizable contingent. Turkey deployed a heavy infantry brigade of six thousand soldiers from 1950 to 1953. A Thai Army regiment fought at the Battle of Pork Chop Hill (October–November 1952) and served with the UNC from 1950 to 1955.

Important Secondary Actors
India, Australia, and Canada

Strategic Military: India and the PRC have a "frozen war" in the Himalayas. India can interdict China's maritime resource supply line from Africa and southwest Asia.

Diplomatic Relationships: Delhi nationalists regard Australians as fellow victims of British imperialism. This positions Australia as India's political interlocutor in defense relationships with Japan and the US Australia is acquiring Aegis ballistic missile defense destroyers. North Korean ICBMs also threaten western Canada.

Taiwan and Vietnam: The PRC claims Taiwan is its missing province. As long as Taiwan (the Republic of China) maintains a separate government, the Chinese Civil War isn't finished. In 1979, the PRC fought a deadly border war with Vietnam and was defeated.

Vietnam continues to maintain a credible military capability. China and Vietnam have several territorial disputes in the Paracel Islands (see chapter three).

Russia: Russia is a major military power. In 1950, in the guise of the USSR, Russia instigated the North Korean attack on South Korea. Russian MiG-15 pilots flew combat missions on behalf of the north—a covert operation (see chapter five on Russian gray-area warfare). Until the mid-1990s, Russia supplied North Korea with weapons and oil.

Wild Card

Iran: Iran has aided North Korea's nuclear weapons and ballistic missile programs. Iran purchased weapons from North Korea.

Ten Knowns

The threat that revived war presents to peace and productivity in East Asia and the Pacific basin is immense. Ten points help explain key issues, define the risks, and identify key actor capabilities.

Known 1: The Korean War survived the Cold War's demise. The military demarcation line (MDL) dividing the United Nations' "truce village" of Panmunjom doesn't legally demarcate the political boundary between North Korea and South Korea. It simply splits the DMZ, separating two warring armies ostensibly observing the fragile ceasefire that the 1953 armistice established. The DMZ more or less reflects the final positions of the dug-in free world and Communist armies (North Korean and Chinese). The armistice agreement says it is an interim arrangement to ensure "a complete cessation of hostilities and of all acts of armed force in Korea until a final peaceful settlement is achieved."

However, as this book goes to press, a final peace settlement does not exist. That means every American president since Harry Truman is a Korean War president. Truman was president in 1950 when, with the backing of Soviet Russia, North Korea's "Great Leader" Kim Il Sung launched a surprise invasion of South Korea. The war Kim 1 began would eventually involve the US and Communist China.

Known 2: The 1953 ceasefire did end the war between the US and Communist China. This is a point always relevant to the Korean problem but also to evolving US–Chinese twenty-first-century relations. The US and China have fought a war in Korea, and determining Korea's political future was the *casus belli*. In Korea, the US learned that China will attack when its borders are threatened. In Korea, China saw the US fight a major war on behalf of a vulnerable Asian ally (South Korea) and an Asian nation that five years earlier had been America's mortal enemy (Japan). China sees these facts as a strong indication that the US will wage war to protect itself and its treaty allies from nuclear attack by the criminal gang in Pyongyang. The economic, political, and military contexts shaping US–Chinese relations have changed dramatically, but close-combat experience taught these major powers that their military personnel fight with fierce determination and a conventional US–Chinese war would be extremely costly and bloody.

Known 3: In terms of economic success, political influence, and cultural vitality, South Korea has completely defeated North Korea. The ROK's 2017 annual gross domestic product (GDP) was around two trillion dollars. A South Korean (Ban Ki-moon) has served as secretary-general of the UN. South Korean entertainers have a global audience. Seoul is a happening place.

Known 4: The US, China, Japan, and South Korea have the first, second, third, and twelfth (respectively) most productive economies on the planet. These nations are trading partners and have common economic interests. As a result, a major war on the Korean peninsula has global economic consequences. An economic depression is conceivable. DPRK GDP data are unreliable. Estimates for its 2013 GDP range from twenty-eight billion dollars to as low as fourteen billion dollars. A 2017 survey of 135 economies ranked North Korea's in the bottom five.

Known 5: Culture, cultural identities, and historical identities count. East Asian ethnic savagery has seeded deep historical and ethno-nationalist resentments that hinder contemporary political relations and cultural interaction. These volatile resentments could ignite the Korean cocktail from hell. For over four centuries, the Imjin War (1592–1598), an embittering conflict that combined an invasion of Korea and inter-ethnic viciousness, has stirred ethnic distrust among the Japanese, Chinese, and Koreans (see "Relevant History"). North and South Koreans despise the Japanese—Tokyo's brutal "integration" policies while Japan ruled Korea as a colony (1905–1945) and WWII sex slavery (Korean "comfort women" servicing Japanese troops) are two poisonous examples. The Chinese despise Japan and the Japanese people—Japan has committed many war crimes against China and the Chinese, with the 1937–1938 Rape of Nanking atrocity being a ghastly example. As for the Koreans and Chinese? China worries that Koreans dream of establishing an independent state based on the kingdom of Goguryeo (first century BC to AD early seventh century). Goguryeo, a proto-Korea (Goryeo), controlled the Korean Peninsula and parts of Manchuria. China's legacy of domination and depredation riles Koreans. The Japanese? The Japanese still regard Koreans as their ethnic inferiors. Twenty-first century Japan, however, needs allies. China's rise to global power and North Korea's belligerence have given the Japanese an appreciation of South Korean military and economic prowess. All regional hatred isn't inter-ethnic. North Korea's brief occupation of South Korea in 1950 left an intra-ethnic wound.

Known 6: South Korea's across-the-board success utterly humiliates North Korea's ruling Kim regime on a very personal level. The personal level matters, since the regime Kim 1 founded has become a hereditary totalitarian Communist dictatorship. Two of Petrarch's enemies of peace, ambition and envy, are definitely relevant (see chapter one).

Known 7: The North Korean regime's violent nature is a key factor in the conflict. Violent threats backed by violent acts maintain Kim regime power. Current dictator Kim Jong Un (Kim 3) purged and then executed his uncle, allegedly using anti-aircraft guns. Kim 3's agents assassinated his half-brother, Kim Jong Nam, by splashing the victim with VX (a nerve agent) at Kuala Lumpur International Airport, Malaysia. The regime relies on repression, murder, and mass atrocities against its own people to maintain power. Mass starvation as a weapon is a calculated domestic political and economic tool. The regime rewards supporters, such as personnel in elite military units, with sufficient food. Feeding "less essential" peasants and workers poor-quality food or starving them saves money to build missiles.

Known 8: In the international arena, threats and episodic acts of "revived" hot war by the DPRK against South Korea and the US have produced economic rewards. South Korea, Japan, the US, and other donors have provided the Kim regime with economic assistance, with the goal of curbing the regime's belligerence. Aid advocates contended that the Kim regime would eventually realize that South Korea and its allies do not seek North Korea's destruction and its behavior would moderate. Instead, the Kim regime turned the "threat and aid" cycle into an extortion racket. South Korea knew a conventional DPRK military attack could badly damage its Seoul. (See "Complexity 1.")

Known 9: Crime—to include violent crime—is a Kim regime foreign policy tool. The regime operates several international crime syndicates that generate hard currency to spend on luxury items for regime elites and weaponry. Per the overview, criminal sovereignty is a form of economic diplomacy.

Known 10: The year 2017 began with the violent, murderous, and criminal Kim regime pursuing operational nuclear weapons and long-range delivery systems (ICBMs) capable of threatening American and Canadian cities. This is a hereditary quest, pursued by Kim 1, Kim 2, and Kim 3. A nuclear warhead on an ICBM gives Kim Jong Un the power to incinerate Los Angeles almost as easily as Seoul.

Six Unknowns

As described in the introduction, unknown unknowns inflict wicked problems.

Unknown 1: Does the Kim regime think it can still win the Korean War? The megalomaniac demand goes like this: "Surrender everything to us right now, or we will ruin the world for everybody." This possibility cannot be ignored. Diplomacy can always falter.

Unknown 2: From Known 10. Some analysts argue the Kim regime's goals are criminal reward and regime survival, not winning the Korean War. Nuclear blackmail to extort cash, however, is a very risky criminal racket. However, payoffs an ideolog would reject might entice a criminal. Would Kim Jong Un sell out for beach condos, K-pop bands, and guarantees an American smart bomb will never descend on his villa?

Unknown 3: Has China fundamentally changed its political relationship with North Korea? This question is the strategic version of several operational unknowns. Here are three: (1) Is China willing to use its economic and diplomatic power to utterly beggar the North Korean state with the goal of de-nuclearizing its ruling regime?; (2) Does China even possess the power to de-nuclearize the Kim regime without resorting to kinetic warfare?; (3) Would China invade North Korea to de-nuclearize it? Would China invade to keep it from collapsing? It appears that Beijing's support for Pyongyang circa 2018 is not as ironclad as its support circa 1961. China ostensibly supports sanctions to force North Korea to de-nuclearize but is routinely caught illicitly supplying the DPRK with critical products and resources. The 1961 date has not been selected randomly. The 1961 mutual assistance treaty between China and North Korea created a bilateral alliance that China described with a colorful narrative trope: two nations as close as "teeth and lips." The treaty gave notice that China intended to maintain a buffer state between its border and US forces in South Korea. The treaty included a provision stating that China and the DPRK could not join another alliance that opposed either party. North Korea could not ally with Russia to oppose China. However, if China were to support the US/

UN mandated total trade embargo, what happens if North Korea accuses China of joining an anti-DPRK alliance?

Unknown 4: Enforcing any peacefully negotiated agreement to de-nuclearize North Korea would require the most thorough and sustained verification regimen in history. North Korea has broken prior inspection agreements. What happens if North Korea balks at mandated inspections after agreeing to permit them? The US also demands "irreversibility." (See US Narrative 2018 and CVID.)

Unknown 5: Would the US attack North Korea to destroy its nuclear weapons and ICBMs without South Korean permission? No, it would not, is the common answer. It's an unknown that troubles Pyongyang. Washington, Seoul, and Tokyo leverage this uncertainty.

Unknown 6: Is China willing to go to war to avert the formation of a united, democratic Korea allied with the US? Beijing leverages this uncertainty.

Relevant Geography and History

The Korean Peninsula is the key communication, trade, and invasion route between mainland Asia and Japan's southern home islands— and "between" is an important word. The Korea Strait connects the East China Sea and the Sea of Japan (which many Koreans insist on calling the East Sea). The strait lies between the Korean Peninsula's southern tip and the Japanese home island of Kyushu. The strait is about 125 miles wide, but scattered islands make it possible for smaller craft to cross the channel. For example, the Japanese island of Tsushima is only thirty miles from the South Korean port of Busan. (Occasionally South Korean politicians claim that Tsushima is Korean territory.)

As Beijing sees it, Chinese control (or suzerain domination) of the peninsula keeps genocidal Japanese imperialists offshore. As Tokyo sees it, Japanese control of the peninsula keeps barbarian Asian invaders well inland. In 1281, the Mongols launched their ill-fated second amphibious assault on Japan from the kingdom of Goryeo (Korea). The Mongols ruled China (founding the Yuan Dynasty in 1271), but the Mongols had made Korea a semi-autonomous vassal for several decades prior.

The 1281 sea invasion failed, thanks to a ship-smashing typhoon which the Japanese called a "divine wind" (*kamikaze).*

Over the centuries, Korea's geographic "between-ness" has forced its leaders to accommodate its powerful island and continental neighbors. Often accommodation meant ceding degrees of internal political authority to Japanese, Chinese, or Russian overlords. Nevertheless, the Korean people fiercely resisted cultural submission and absorption by foreign powers.

The Imjin War (1592–1598) was the biggest East Asian international conflict of its era. Japanese warlord Toyotomi Hideyoshi wanted to conquer China and dominate Asia. His samurai supporters wanted land and plunder. "Between-ness" took him through Korea. Ming Dynasty China allied with Korea. Chinese troops, however, killed both Koreans and Japanese. Koreans regarded Chinese soldiers as armed thugs. Korean forces eventually defeated the Japanese invaders. Memories of the sixteenth-century ethnic slaughter linger.

The Korean War

In the last weeks of World War II, the USSR entered the war against Japan. Soviet forces invaded Manchuria. On August 10, 1945, Soviet

29

forces entered Korea and stopped their advance at the 38th parallel, per an agreement with the US

The USSR and Mao's Red Chinese forces supported Korea's Communist Party, led by Kim Il Sung. The USSR began providing the North Korean Communists with weapons, supplies, and training. Japan's surrender left Korea split in half, with Communists in the north and US forces in the south. As Cold War competition intensified, two Korean governments emerged, a pro-US government in the south (Syngman Rhee became its first president in August 1948) and a Communist government in the north (formed by Kim Il Sung and declared in September 1948). Both posed as Korea's legitimate government.

On June 25, 1950, North Korean Communist soldiers invaded the south and overran South Korea's poorly equipped forces. North Korea announced that its soldiers had orders to kill the "bandit traitor" Syngman Rhee. On June 28, the Communists seized Seoul. With a well-trained tank regiment leading the attack, North Korean forces raced south toward the port of Busan on the Korea Strait. America's Truman administration concluded the defense of Japan depended upon defending South Korea. Air attacks, naval gunfire, and a handful of ground units brought piecemeal from Japan (the ill-fated Task Force Smith, a battalion-sized unit, was the most memorable) slowed the north's advance as US and South Korean forces established a defensive perimeter around Busan. The Communist siege of the "Pusan Perimeter" became a stalemate.

An American-led counteroffensive began in September 1950, featuring an amphibious assault at Inchon, the port west of Seoul. The UN command's offensive routed North Korean forces and took Seoul in late September. On October 1, UN forces crossed the 38th parallel, and on October 10 took Pyongyang. Despite Chinese warnings, American forces continued north, approaching the North Korean–Chinese border.

Then US forces got too close (see Known 2). In late October, Chinese Communist soldiers began infiltrating North Korea and occupying concealed positions. On November 2, 1950, the Chinese Communist People's Liberation Army invaded North Korea in force and attacked dispersed US units that were pursuing defeated North Korean soldiers. The Americans were routed. US and other UN forces retreated south of Pyongyang and then withdrew to positions near the 38th parallel. In January 1951, Chinese forces captured Seoul. The UN command counterattacked and liberated Seoul in March 1951. From that point forward, ground fighting seesawed, with the 38th parallel being the approximate pivot.

The July 1953 armistice found the US worrying about a nuclear attack—spurred by the USSR's acquisition of nuclear weapons. The American people saw the Korean conflict as a no-win war. The Chinese Communist Army was utterly exhausted. Several "shot-out" Chinese divisions fielded fewer than a thousand soldiers. A ceasefire made sense.

August 1953: From the DMZ to Busan, South Korea lay in ruins. Rubble choked its shattered cities. Wretched South Korea, now one of the world's poorest countries, faced starvation. North Korea had suffered heavy damage. Kim Il Sung, however, remained its Great Leader.

The war continued in a gray zone. The DMZ Conflict is a collective name, a unifying retrospective title for a series of small battles, raids, and attempted assassinations that occurred from October 1966 to October 1969. Many of these combat engagements occurred near the DMZ. The DMZ area firefights were, typically, ambushes, failed infiltration operations, or some combination of the two in which North Koreans would infiltrate and ambush South Korean and American soldiers south of the DMZ, or American or South Korean soldiers would detect and fire upon northern infiltrators. For example, on November 2, 1966, North Korean infiltrators ambushed a US 2nd Infantry Division patrol south of the DMZ, killing six US soldiers and one South Korean. On April 5, 1967, American soldiers manning a 2nd Infantry Division post south of the DMZ spotted infiltrating North Koreans, fired on them, and killed five. On April 29, 1967, a 2nd Infantry Division patrol south of the DMZ detected and ambushed North Korean infiltrators, killing one and capturing one. The DMZ Conflict cost South Korea 299 dead and 550 wounded. Forty-three Americans were killed and 111 wounded.

Three Korean Tactical, Operational, and Strategic Complexities to Ponder

Complexity 1: North Korea's Tactical Fixing Force: DMZ Conventional Artillery Threat to Seoul

Greater Seoul is an economic powerhouse with a GDP exceeding one trillion dollars and some twenty-five million inhabitants. Seoul's bright lights burn less than thirty-five miles from the DMZ. Its proximity has always made it vulnerable to North Korean conventional attack; urban sprawl has made it more so. The last stop on Seoul's metro is about six miles from the DMZ's southern edge, which illustrates the area's vulnerability to North Korean conventional artillery fire.

The terrain on the DPRK side of the DMZ features hills and ridges. North Korea has used the past six decades to fortify the region with bunkers, reinforced tunnels, underground supply depots, and HARTS—hardened artillery sites. These sites usually consist of a tunnel hiding the artillery system (tube artillery or rocket launcher). Some include a protected firing position. HARTS are located as close to the DMZ's northern boundary as terrain and concealment permit. Analysts believe most HARTS are within six to twelve miles of the DMZ, though some are closer. The DMZ has a width of about two and a half miles, which means it is not much of a buffer.

North Korea's tactical scheme is simple: the artillery piece exits the tunnel, fires a volley south, then rolls back inside its fort.

Goyang, Gimpo, Uijeongbu, and Yangju are ROK towns located within twenty to twenty-five miles of suspected HARTS. Tube and rocket artillery in these HARTS could batter the Seoul region with thousands of tons of explosives per hour. Some artillery pieces can fire chemical munitions (the nerve agents VX and sarin are in North Korea's chemical arsenal).

North Korea has built several hundred troop bunkers near the DMZ. The larger bunkers supposedly contain enough military equipment to arm up to 1500 soldiers. The implication: Pyongyang could launch a quick assault on Seoul with anywhere from five to ten forward-deployed infantry divisions. North Korea has dug tunnels beneath the DMZ capable of supporting this type of surprise infantry strike south.

The tactical-level military combination—infantry, tactical weapons, and logistical and engineering preparations—is more powerful than the sum of its military parts. The ability to threaten South Korea's economic hub with a destructive conventional attack gives North Korea non-nuclear strategic diplomatic leverage.

Or it has. In the past, Seoul's conventional vulnerability has indeed limited the South Korean government's freedom of action when responding to violent North Korea provocations.

However, South Korea is employing new technology to counter North Korea's conventional threat as well as counter its missile arsenal. Small UAVs and other remote surveillance and targeting systems are identifying and monitoring static HART locations, bunkers, tunnels, and missile launch sites. Static is a vulnerability—artillery can move, but HARTS can't. However, unprotected artillery must face allied firepower. South Korea and Japan have acquired advanced smart weapons that complement American firepower. Armed with an array of warheads (to include deep penetrating "bunker busters") and guided by targeting systems permitting attack from any direction, these advanced smart weapons make North Korean HARTS and other static structures vulnerable to suppression (the weapon cannot deploy to fire) and destruction (the weapon is destroyed, and perhaps the site, as well). North Korea's conventional threat to Seoul may be diminishing.

Complexity 2: North Korean Shock Lethality Operations

North Korea's shock lethality operations include unprovoked conventional military attacks, terror, and assassination attempts. Here are some examples:

January 21, 1968, Blue House Raid: On January 17, thirty-one North Korean commandos assigned to North Korea's elite Unit 124 assassination team infiltrated South Korea with the mission of assassinating South Korean president Park Chung Hee. Civilians spotted them in transit and reported their presence. However, the commandos evaded South Korean security units and entered Seoul disguised as

South Korean soldiers. The team was detected as it approached the Blue House, the president's residence. The team fired on Blue House security personnel and fled Seoul to rally points in the mountains (one located north of Seoul near Uijeongbu). South Korean Army units pursued and engaged the commandos in several small but deadly firefights, the last occurring on January 29. South Korea suffered twenty-six killed and sixty-six wounded (two dozen South Korean casualties were civilians). Twenty-nine Unit 124 commandos were slain, one was captured alive, and one successfully returned to North Korea.

January 23, 1968, USS *Pueblo* Incident: North Korea seized the US navy intelligence ship *Pueblo* in international waters. One US sailor died. Eighty-two sailors were imprisoned for eleven months.

April 15, 1969, EC-121 Incident: North Korea shot down an unarmed American EC-121 recon plane over the East Sea (Sea of Japan). All thirty-one Americans aboard died.

August 18, 1976, Axe Murders/Poplar Tree Incident: American and South Korean soldiers were trimming tree branches in the neutral Joint Security Area (JSA) of Panmunjom. North Korean soldiers attacked with axes and murdered two U.S. Army officers. The attackers wounded nine other American and Korean soldiers.

October 9, 1983, Rangoon Assassination Bombing: North Korean agents tried to assassinate South Korean president Chun Doo Hwan using a bomb. Chun was visiting Rangoon, Burma (Myanmar). He survived, but the explosion killed four Burmese and seventeen South Korean government officials. Forty-six other people were wounded.

November 29, 1987, Terror Bomb Downs Korean Air Flight 858: North Korean operatives placed a bomb on a South Korean civilian flight. The bomb downed the plane, killing its 115 passengers.

March 26, 2010, North Korea Sinks South Korea's *Cheonan*: A mysterious explosion south of the West Sea's NLL sank the South Korean Navy corvette *Cheonan*. Forty-six sailors were killed out of a crew of 104. International investigators concluded that a North Korean torpedo sank the *Cheonan*.

November 23, 2010, Artillery Attack on Yeonpyeong Island: A North Korean rocket artillery battery on the mainland launched a surprise attack on South Korea's Yeonpyeong Island. South Korean Marine artillery on the island returned fire; the exchange lasted an hour. North Korean fire killed two South Korean civilians and two Marines. Three civilians and fifteen Marines were wounded.

February 13, 2017, Assassination of Kim Jong Nam: Assassins working for Kim Jong Un murdered his half-brother, Kim Jong Nam, at Kuala Lumpur International Airport, Malaysia. They used the liquid nerve agent VX, an illegal WMD. At one time, Kim Jong Nam was believed to be Kim Jong Il's designated heir. Some North Korean expatriate organizations had urged Kim Jong Nam to encourage political modernization in North Korea.

Complexity 3: The Sad, Failed Case of Strategic Sunshine

Various South Korean, Japanese, and American administrations have used "soft power" appeals to encourage North Korean good behavior and solicit cooperation. Soft power advocates argued that giving Pyongyang "carrots" would eventually reduce its aggressiveness.

The Clinton administration's 1994 Agreed Framework gave Kim Il Sung heavy fuel oil and technical assistance if his regime would shut down the nuclear reactors it was using to produce weapons-grade plutonium. The US would even help North Korea acquire light water nuclear reactors for electrical generation if it permitted

International Atomic Energy Agency inspections and complied with other IAEA safeguards. In 2002, the US determined that North Korea had violated the Agreed Framework and had an ongoing uranium enrichment program.

In 1998, South Korea began its Sunshine Policy. South Korea would reward North Korea with economic incentives in exchange for political cooperation. Seoul sought détente and peace.

In 2002 (the Sunshine Policy's apogee), Seoul formally proposed creating the Kaesong Industrial Region. Seoul would finance a cooperative manufacturing park in North Korean territory, about six miles above the DMZ. Southern managers and business teams could commute from Seoul. South Korea would supply power and water. In Kaesong, South Korean managerial expertise and manufacturing technology would combine with North Korean labor to benefit both Koreas.

In 2006, North Korea conducted its first nuclear test. A frightened South Korea demanded that the north halt its nuclear program. Pyongyang refused.

In 2008, the South Korean government decided to curb its Sunshine Policy. Some incentive programs would continue; however, there would be no new programs until North Korea ceased its nuclear quest. In 2008, the North responded by testing another nuke. The *Cheonan* incident solidified opposition to the Sunshine Policy. In November 2010, South Korea's Ministry of Unification terminated Sunshine entirely.

South Korea continued to maintain Kaesong. North Korea, however, treated the zone like an economic hostage. (The Kim regime allegedly skimmed seventy percent of Kaesong worker salaries.) In 2009, Pyongyang canceled Kaesong's wage and rent agreements, then demanded pay increases for North Korean workers. In April 2013, North Korea shuttered Kaesong. When it reopened five months later, South Korean companies operating Kaesong facilities had lost approximately one billion dollars.

Through 2015, Kaesong employed around 54,000 North Koreans. On January 6, 2016, Pyongyang tested another nuclear device. South Korea and Japan warned the North that further missile tests would have consequences. On February 7, North Korea fired a missile.

On February 10, South Korea withdrew its citizens from Kaesong, closing the facility. The Sunshine Policy's "soft power" approach had failed to stop North Korea's nuclear weapons program.

Military-Security Worries, Diplomatic Goals, and Narratives
North Korea

For three decades, the Kim regime has faced four critical issues: (1) its own survival (regime maintenance), (2) North Korea's economic decline and ruin, (3) ensuring Chinese support in confrontations with South Korea and the US, and (4) the need to occasionally adjust its relationship with South Korea. Issues 2, 3, and 4 directly affect issue 1.

Byongjin Military Economics: In 2013, Kim Jong Un announced his "Byongjin" policy (byongjin doctrine) of seeking nuclear armament and economic growth. *Byongjin* is a word that translates as "simultaneous push." Byongjin definitely modified Kim Jong Il's "Songun" ("military first") policy that gave the North Korean military political authority and priority on the allocation of resources. Kim 3's policy implicitly recognized that military power alone did not assure regime survival. North Korea must revive economically. At the time, analysts speculated Kim 3 would allow North Korea's informal economy to grow. North Korea's informal economy of streetside stalls and unofficial markets (*jangmadang*) has expanded. In 2017, a South Korean source estimated the informal economy produced seventy percent of North Korean household income. In theory, the tandem of economic growth and deliverable nuclear weapons would protect the regime. However, the nuclear weapons quest resulted in aggressive American and South Korean pushback, to include crippling economic sanctions. As of 2018, the sanctions have crippled Kim 3's limited economic experiment.

Nuclear Narrative Warfare: Korea's major export is the threat of war magnified by potential nuclear holocaust—a threat narrative backed by nuclear weapons. It's an international version of an alley bully's extortion game. "Pay me off," the punk waving the pistol says, "or I'll burn down your store." The analogy, however, goes only so far. North Korea's Kim waves a nuclear weapon.

But if he uses it, he kills himself, so war's edge is the goal, not war's abyss. North Korea needs economic aid, so the regime seeks a payoff. Even if food, fuel, and other forms of aid are not forthcoming, North Korea craves recognition. A month or so with Pyongyang in the global spotlight may be a sufficient political reward. Pyongyang cherishes this theatrical narrative: Fearless North Korea has the courage to confront rich and powerful nations such as the U.S., South Korea, Japan—and perhaps even China.

Military Economics and Conventional Military Decline: North Korea's conventional military capabilities have declined in comparison to South Korean and Japanese capabilities. North Korea's tank force is largely obsolete and its air force is a relic. Defectors report that elite military units are poorly fed, stockpiled ammunition (small arms and artillery) is dated and unreliable, and vehicles lack parts. Defectors also report low morale in military units. That has to worry the Kim regime.

Another WMD Military Option: Even if it de-nuclearizes, North Korea could threaten South Korea and Japan with other weapons of mass destruction (WMD). North Korea has chemical weapons (such as the nerve agent VX) that can be delivered in artillery shells and missile warheads.

South Korea

South Korea's cultural clout and economic success make it clear which Korea won the war for enjoying life. The world knows it. South Korea knows the world knows it. Which leads to a primary domestic political goal: South Korea wants to enjoy its wealth without fear of North Korean savagery and nuclear destruction.

Tailored Retaliation: The *Cheonan* sinking in 2010 affected South Korean policy. Seoul will no longer tolerate North Korean acts of intimidation. In 2013, the South Korean government issued its own set of intra-Korean rules. It would meet Pyongyang provocations with diplomatic deftness and military might. The South was prepared to escalate a "situation." Seoul calls this policy "tailored retaliation."

Military Operation with a Narrative: South Korea has formulated two military operational concepts for deterring or ending North Korea's nuclear threat. "Kill Chain" is a South Korean preemptive strike concept in which an array of surveillance, intelligence, and reconnaissance capabilities directly connect to conventional attack systems (aircraft, bombs, cruise and ballistic missiles, rockets, and the like). The conventional systems rely heavily on smart weapons and very high-speed missiles. For example, South Korea has armed its F-15K Slam Eagle strike fighters with advanced high-speed, air-launched missiles. The missiles have a range of over 150 miles and can carry a variety of warheads. The weapons can destroy missile launch sites and launchers. They also threaten North Korean command facilities. South Korea would implement Kill Chain if intelligence determines a North Korean attack is imminent (especially a missile attack). Kill Chain systems would attack North Korean artillery positions along the DMZ. (See the conclusion of Complexity 1.) The second concept is the Korea Massive Punishment and Retaliation (KMPR) plan. This plan targets senior members of the North Korean regime for elimination. KMPR uses a range of weapons, including special forces units in "decapitation" attacks (assassinations). The narrative directed at North Korean elites: We can kill you where you live, and we know where you live.

Narrative and Cultural Warfare: South Korean popular entertainment is a weapon North Korea can no longer close the electronic gates on. Two recent North Korean defectors, both soldiers, praised South Korean K-pop music, especially marquee K-pop girl band acts. South Korean information operations spotlight North Korean military defector testimony.

Possible Diplomatic Operation: South Korea might assure China that if Korean unification occurred, American troops (should any remain) would never have bases north of the DMZ.

Japan

Japan is increasingly assertive militarily and diplomatically. Domestic reluctance to use military power has declined. Japan fears North Korean nukes, but ultimately, Japan is far more concerned about China's growing power than it is about North Korea's.

Diplomatic and Military Non-Starter: Japan will not trade its improving and expanding missile defense systems for North Korean nuclear weapons.

Diplomatic Narrative Warfare and Possible Military Operation: Japan possesses a robust civilian nuclear industry and first-class manufacturing industries. Japanese defense officials have referred to Japan's commercial reactors as a tacit nuclear deterrent. In April 2016, the government said that Japan's constitution does not forbid nuclear weapons. Both statements send a diplomatic and military message. If pressed by North Korea or China, Japan could develop nuclear weapons within four to ten months. Some analysts speculate Japan has built critical component parts. Whatever the case, Tokyo could build a bomb quickly.

China

For China, North Korea's nuclear quest affects two critical defense issues: (1) Japanese and South Korean nuclearization. China fears that Japan and South Korea will use North Korea as an excuse to acquire their own nuclear weapons; and (2) twenty-first-century containment. Chinese strategists argue that the US, Japan, and South Korea are using the crisis to establish a stronger military alliance with the long-term goal of containing China (see chapter three).

Strategic Diplomatic and Military Goals: China wants a buffer state between its borders and American forces. A North Korean regime collapse would threaten that strategic objective and create other security problems. China saw the Kim regime mishandle North Korea's 1990s' economic catastrophe. That debacle included a famine that killed over five percent of the DPRK's population. Beijing concluded a North Korean government implosion would threaten the security of China's northeastern provinces, particularly those bordering North Korea. A refugee invasion is another concern. Beijing knows a "humanitarian" invasion (the H in DIMEFILCH) is a security issue. A refugee crisis could seed chaos throughout China and threaten Communist Party control in Beijing. If North Korea's Communists can fall, why not China's?

Military Option in North Korea: Some analysts take it as a given that if the Kim regime implodes, Chinese forces would enter North Korea to restore order. It is an option, related to Unknown 6. Intervention would likely deter South Korean intervention and the formation of another united, democratic Korea allied with the US

An Anti-US Diplomatic-Economic Operation: China could undercut US de-nuclearization efforts with the goal of embarrassing Washington and demonstrating the limits of American power and influence. Covertly evading economic sanctions is one method. Undermining US influence in the Asia-Pacific region serves long-range Chinese strategic goals (see chapter three). China has employed this Korea narrative and could use it again: Troubles on the Korean peninsula is a bilateral US-North Korea problem and the result of aggressive American policies. This narrative portrays North Korean missile and nuclear programs as defensive.

Possible Diplomatic-Military Initiative to Promote Denuclearization: Offer the Kim regime "extended deterrence" (protection by Chinese nuclear weapons) in exchange for North Korean denuclearization.

Possible Diplomatic Narrative Operation to Divide the US–South Korea–Japan Alliance and Advance Long-Range Goals: Offer to trade North Korean de-nuclearization for the removal of South Korea and Japanese missile defense systems.

United States

When coordinating policy to achieve a goal, such as de-nuclearizing the Korean Peninsula, the South Korea–U.S.–Japan combination wields immense economic and political power backed by modern military forces. The PRC respects it.

As this book is written, Washington has publicly stated that North Korea has achieved its goal of building ICBMs capable of striking the United States. North Korea's improved IRBMs can already reach Guam, parts of Alaska, and Hawaii.

As of 2018, the US and its democratic allies, South Korea and Japan, are not demanding a regime change. North Korea's vicious regime can continue to run a Stalinist gulag. This diplomatic position, regime survival, is designed to encourage the Kim regime to negotiate and denuclearize. It is also a concession to China. If the North Korean gulag remains, Communist China will retain an authoritarian and semi-dependent buffer prison state between its border and South Korea. If permitting regime survival fails to produce denuclearization, regime destruction is an alternative.

US Narrative 2018: North Korea has gone too far. The US will never allow the North to obtain nuclear weapons that threaten Guam, Hawaii, and North America (US and Canada). The US summarizes its demand as Complete, Verifiable, and Irreversible De-nuclearization (CVID). The operations required to assure "verifiability" and "irreversibility" would be highly intrusive, but the alternative is war.

The US also wants North Korea to destroy its long-range nuclear delivery systems (ICBMs).

A real-world event reinforces this American demand. In January 2018, a false warning that Honolulu was under missile attack demonstrated that rational people fear nuclear-armed missiles, especially when malign regimes threaten such attacks.

Sketching a Muscular American DIMEFILCH Cocktail

The Trump Administration's North Korea Denuclearization Operations, 2017–2018 (Twenty-First Century Multi-Dimensional Coercive Diplomacy)

This "first brush" narrative describes ongoing history. This sub-section records illustrative events that occurred from March 2017 to March 2018 are accurate. They are an example of a concerted effort to wage twenty-first-century "cocktail" warfare. Subsequent events will determine the effectiveness of this multi-dimensional operation.

The Coercive Diplomacy narrative actually begins with Donald Trump's October 24, 1999 *Meet the Press* interview with Tim Russert. The interview is a historically illuminating flash forward to his administration's 2017–2018 "de-nuclearizing" North Korea coercive diplomatic effort. It also adds convincing depth to the US narrative that "North Korea has gone too far."

Based on administration statements made in 2017, "de-nuclearizing" means destroying the DPRK's nukes and its long-range missile delivery systems. If coercive diplomacy does not produce this result, a war would, though with hideously destructive costs.

In the 1999 interview, Trump summarizes the American government's weak responses to North Korea's slow but undeterred quest for nuclear weapons:

First I'd negotiate and be sure I could get the best deal possible.... The biggest problem this world has is nuclear proliferation. And we have a country out there in North Korea which is sort of wacko, which is not a bunch of dummies, and they are developing nuclear weapons.... If that negotiation doesn't work, then better solve the problem now than solve it later. (Trump 1999)

A narrative warfare gambit? Given the twentieth-century date, the statement was either bravado or a promise to act when and if. The Trump administration's subsequent actions demonstrate Trump made a promise. In March 2017, Trump's foreign policy began a coordinated attack on Kim Jong Un's regime with the interim goals of disrupting Pyongyang's political and military plans, exposing the regime's grave weaknesses, and psychologically rattling its leader. The administration's ultimate goal was to set conditions to de-nuclearize the Korean Peninsula.

On March 17, 2017, then-Secretary of State Rex Tillerson declared, "The policy of strategic patience has ended. We are exploring a new range of diplomatic, security, economic measures. All options are on the table." He added that if North Korea didn't end its nuclear weapons and ballistic missile programs, why, Japan and South Korea might have to acquire their own nuclear arsenals.

That same month Tillerson said the first steps to coerce de-nuclearization would be additional UN sanctions. Regarding China, Tillerson said, with diplomatic finesse, "No one issue defines the relationship between the US and China. We will be talking about a broad range of issues when I'm in Beijing. But the threat of North Korea is imminent. And it has reached a level that we are very concerned about the consequences of North Korea being allowed to continue on this progress it's been making on the development of both weapons and delivery systems."

Declaring North Korea an imminent threat was a dire warning—diplomatic finesse moved to dire warning. Diplomacy implied kinetic military action. American economic power, however, would be the primary instrument.

Tillerson's rejection of strategic patience was an explicit repudiation of the Obama-era policy as expressed by Secretary of State Hillary Clinton, the Democrat presidential candidate in 2016: "The approach that our administration is taking is of strategic patience in close coordination with our six-party allies." Recall the Sunshine Policy and other "soft power" initiatives had failed, and this was evident during the Obama administration. (See Complexity 3.)

In April 2017, Vice President Mike Pence visited South Korea and assured the country, "We [Americans] are one hundred percent with you." Pence said North Korea's economic and political isolation is what the nuclearization is predicated upon. Complete economic isolation would deny North Korea all imports and stop its exports. The coercive diplomatic operation that vice president Pence sketched solicited collective international economic and diplomatic action to end the threat of nuclear war in East Asia.

The Trump administration made it clear North Korea bore responsibility for the horrors that are and the horrors that could be. However, China, pursuing its policy of strategic ambiguity, has served as Pyongyang's key enabler.

However, China and Russia border North Korea; isolation of the Kim regime is impossible without their cooperation.

In April 2017, the Trump administration suggested that China would receive a favorable trade deal—and perhaps other unspecified considerations—if Beijing helped terminate North Korea's nuclear weapons program. (See chapter three for a discussion of China's economic goals and potential vulnerabilities.) A de-nuclearized peninsula would signal to China that the US was guaranteeing that China would not confront a nuclear-armed South Korea. Should North Korea collapse and South Korea absorb it, the reunified Korea would not possess nukes.

US, South Korean, and Japanese military exercises near North Korea began to intensify.

In June 2017, at the Shangri-La summit in Singapore, Secretary of Defense James Mattis said the US had vital interests in the Asian littoral and that the Asia-Pacific region was "a priority region" for Washington. The Trump administration would address regional issues through "military partnerships, robust investment and trade relationships, and close ties between the peoples of our countries."

Then he addressed North Korea's "clear intent" to acquire nuclear-armed missiles. Mattis said he believed China would "come to recognize North Korea as a strategic liability, not an asset." Mattis said the US would "engage China diplomatically and economically to ensure our relationship is beneficial." That was a carrot.

But Mattis didn't shy away from confronting China's South China Sea aggression. He declared that the 2016 arbitration court ruling concluding that China had illegally seized Filipino territory was binding and served as a diplomatic starting point to peacefully manage regional disputes. That was careful, measured language—in effect, "Let's play by the rules and respect each other."

As he finished, Mattis mentioned, as if in passing, that for the first time the US would give Vietnam a retired US Coast Guard cutter. That was a small but forceful stick waved at Beijing. In 1979, China and Vietnam fought a bloody border war and China lost. China fears a US-Vietnam alliance (see chapter three).

Finally, Mattis said America remained "committed to working with Taiwan and with its democratic government to provide the defense articles necessary…." That's a stick.

Beijing says Taiwan is a breakaway province. Mattis's remark echoed a phone call Trump made to Taiwanese president Tsai Ing-wen in December 2016, shortly after Trump's election.

September 3, 2017: North Korea tested a powerful nuclear device.

On September 23, Trump issued an executive order that informed analysts called a declaration of economic war on North Korea. The order supported Tillerson's warning that the Trump administration would exert maximum pressure on North Korea until the criminal state de-nuclearized. Economic pressure followed diplomatic pressure.

The military pressure included US Air Force strategic bombers flying show-of-force missions around the peninsula, including a foray into international airspace over the East Sea off North Korea's coast.

The pressure also included psychological (Information) pressure on "Little Rocket Man"—Kim Jong Un. Trump coined that *nomme de insult* in September, and it was a useful punch. Trump's nicknames are such damningly effective caricatures that they become psychological weapons. Insulting a dictator's dignity is a potentially valuable psychological weapon. Dictators demonstrate invulnerability by silencing and suppressing dissent and opposition using physical intimidation and coercion, to include mass murder. Kim's inability to stop Trump's taunts or top his taunts demonstrate a kind of vulnerability on Kim's part. Vulnerable dictators don't remain in power, not for long.

On March 5, 2018, Kim Jong Un said he was willing to do something he had said he would never do: discuss de-nuclearizing his regime. He made no demand of South Korea and the US, other than that they meet to discuss the subject face-to-face. A day later, a South Korean delegation met with Kim in Pyongyang and reported that Kim himself had said he understood that South Korean and American joint military drills would continue. That was a huge concession. For decades, the Communist state's propagandists have portrayed allied military exercises as preparations for invading the north. The dictatorship also agreed to suspend its provocative nuclear weapons tests and missile tests while talks continued.

Late June 2018: The March 2018 North Korean concession led to more discussions between South Korea and North Korea and meetings between President Moon and Kim Jong Un. The Trump administration said President Trump and Kim could discuss de-nuclearization face to face but there would be no US and allied concessions. Singapore would host their historic summit. As the summit approached, North Korea tried to alter the diplomatic ground rules. Trump canceled the summit—coercive diplomacy met with coercive diplomacy. North Korea asked the US to hold the Singapore summit. It took place on June 12, 2018. At the summit Trump dropped the "bad cop, good cop," shook hands with the dictator, praised Kim for wisely choosing to talk, and assured him that he and his nation had a safe and wealthy future—as long as Kim followed through on his promise to completely, verifiably, and irreversibly de-nuclearize (CVID). During face-to-face discussions, Trump added another stroke of unpredictable diplomacy: he produced an iPad and showed Kim a four-minute video prepared by the White House. Slickly calculated to fascinate its target audience, the thirty-something movie-loving Kim, the video contained imagery and audio inspired by science fiction films, dramatic historical documentaries, razzle-dazzle adventure video games, and advertisements selling expensive high-tech products. The imagery and audio narration explicitly advocated making responsible decisions that positively shape the future by avoiding destructive nuclear war and promoting wealth. However, in the perspective of the deadly politics behind the summit, the video implicitly condemned Kim's "Byongjin" policy. North Korea could not possess nuclear weapons and have wealth; nuclear weapons guaranteed North Korea's ruin.

The video was a remarkable example of a psychological warfare diplomatic weapon that is simultaneously persuasive and coercive. In street lingo, the psychological cocktail sent this message: "Stay alive and get rich, kid."

As the summit concluded, Kim indicated he would de-nuclearize and Trump responded with a goodwill gesture: South Korean-US military exercises would be suspended as long as North Korea pursued CVID. Like other allied gestures, the exercise suspension could be quickly reversed.

Time will tell if the Trump administration's diplomatic operation de-nuclearizes North Korea and the world avoids a major war. As I finish this book, human history and the American effort both continue. Elements of a serviceable CVID deal have emerged. North Korean domestic media have mentioned the possibility—but the deal has yet to be made. Whatever its outcome, the coordinated coercive diplomatic operation as implemented March 2017 through March 2018 and into June 2018 with the Singapore summit was a remarkable example of a DIMEFILCH cocktail.

Diplomatic and Military Scenarios

What happens if the allies and North Korea fail to reach a CVID deal and peace talks collapse? This list is illustrative, not comprehensive. The scenarios are speculations, not predictions.

1. **Pleading with Beijing to "do the right thing":** China has vulnerabilities. China's imperial territorial expansion in the South China Sea has produced adverse reactions. China's other borders are not problem-free (see chapter three). Eighty-five to ninety percent of North Korea's international trade is with China. North Korea's miserable economy depends on China.

2. **Coercive diplomacy directed at China:** Trade politics and geo-politics frame the US-China relationship. Business isn't simply business when the promise of wealth keeps China's Communist Party in power. Here is a point up for strategic debate: Until China's domestic economy modernizes and its GDP roughly equals America's, America has the economic power to damage China economically and politically. Here are some reasons the argument has merit: The US is energy independent and China is not. The US and its allies can restrict Chinese exports and access to raw materials. Restriction includes naval embargoes. The US Navy is a crack force and the People's Liberation Army Navy (PLAN) is untested. Coercive diplomacy would stop when China forces North Korea to de-nuclearize.

3. **The cynical trade and sellout:** The US, Japan, and South Korea could acknowledge Chinese control of the South China Sea, or they could give Taiwan to China in exchange for a de-nuclearized North Korea.

   Outrageous? Yes. India would never accept it. Indonesia, the Philippines, Vietnam, Singapore, and Australia would go tilt.

4. **Decapitation of the North Korean regime: Assassination intrigues many commentators. However, uncertainties make this a high-risk option.** Targeting Kim Jong Un with a missile or aircraft-delivered munitions is extremely difficult. A commando team breaching his personal security force is farfetched. Moreover, his death may not lead to de-nuclearization, and attacking him would be an act of war. Is there a faction within the North Korean Army willing to stage a military coup? If the theoretical faction were to succeed in removing the Kim regime, would it agree to de-nuclearize? An assassination attempt could be a prelude to a Chinese invasion.

5. **China invades North Korea to de-nuclearize the Kim regime and maintain a compliant buffer state:** Analysts doubt that China would try this unless it had a Trojan horse in the form of a North Korean Army unit or high senior military officer capable of stalling North Korean defensive operations.

6. **Delayed reprisal and the war to de-nuclearize:** Is a preemptive strike reckless? This begs another question: Just how responsible is a belated counterstrike?

   North Korea has committed atrocities throughout Asia. Its regime has murdered and kidnapped South Koreans, Japanese, and Americans. Its embedded belligerency defies the laws of war. A narrative warfare wager might frame the war to de-nuclearize as a delayed reprisal instead of a preemptive strike.

   The US and South Korea have exercised what they call a four-dimensional strategy to detect, defend against, disrupt, and destroy North Korean missiles. Weapons systems involved in the exercises include various US and South Korean aircraft and ships armed with cruise missiles.

The allies could stage a simultaneous strategic bombing strike to knock out North Korean missiles, missile launchers, storage sites, nuclear and chemical weapons sites, command and control centers, communications systems, and airspace defenses.

The US and its allies in East Asia have the aircraft and missiles (ballistic as well as cruise) to deliver at least two thousand (likely more) precision conventional weapons within a two to ten minute time frame on North Korea's critical targets.

A simultaneous strategic bombing strike seeks to surprise the enemy, destroy his strategic weapons systems, and suppress his key defenses throughout the battle area. That is asking a lot—perhaps too much.

Success depends on many things, but the first "D"—detect— is vital. The bombing strike requires very accurate, real-time intelligence. Allied ABMs must be ready to intercept any North Korean missiles that survive the attack.

That's a sketch of the first ten minutes. Over the next month, subsequent strikes would occur to eliminate North Korea's long-range missiles, chemical munitions, nuclear weapons stockpiles, missile manufacturing capabilities, and nuclear weapons manufacturing capabilities.

The US and its allies must protect Seoul. North Korea's tube and rocket artillery systems—even the ones in caves and bunkers—are vulnerable to weapons such as the Massive Ordnance Air Blast and small smart bombs. Smart bombs can close tunnel entrances. (See Complexity 1.)

The assured destruction of North Korean nuclear weapons sites would require an invasion by ground forces. That could produce massive casualties, especially if surviving pro-Kim regime forces used chemical and biological weapons.

CHAPTER 3

THE DRAGON REVIVES

Great Power Collision in the South China Sea

As the second decade of the twenty-first century ends, China is an awkward amalgamation of great success and enormous stress—a simultaneously promising yet dangerous political combination, internally and internationally.

China's four-decade rise from hunger-plagued developing country to Great Power with global clout ranks as one of history's more striking political-economic achievements. The Chinese dragon is back with fire in its belly—that is one narrative. Dragon revivalist narrators employed by Beijing, however, say little or nothing about distressing subjects such as China's demographic challenges, its corrupt elites, its weak and murky judicial system, and the Chinese Communist Party's insistent repression of demands for domestic political liberalization.

Despite these systemic weaknesses—and they are grave ills, especially when they infect a Great Power—Beijing's Communist neo-nationalists crow that two centuries of Chinese decline have reversed. The government's willingness to use its diplomatic, information, military, and economic powers to expand Chinese influence demonstrate that fact.

China's expansion has three general axes. China's Belt and Road Initiative (BRI, formerly called One Belt One Road) is a potent twenty-first century political-economic cocktail with two axes of advance: a thrust west by land and a thrust south, then west, by sea.

The third axis is also maritime, driving east to (and through) Taiwan, toward Japan, to the open Pacific Ocean and beyond. Since 1949, when the Communists defeated the Chinese Nationalists and they fled to Taiwan, Beijing has made it clear the PRC intends to seize the island.

The land "Belt" of the BRI, the land axis of advance, extends from China west through Central Asia to Europe and Southwest Asia, notionally recreating the old Silk Road (at least "Silk" is the political narrative spun by Beijing).

The maritime "Road" of the BRI dives south from mainland China, through the South China Sea (SCS) toward Singapore and the strait leading to the Indian Ocean, the Strait of Malacca. The maritime "Road" then heads west through the Indian Ocean to Africa and the Suez Canal. (See the sub-section China's BRI Cocktail.)

Expanding influence is one thing, territorial expansion, another. People may accept influence—if the influencer pays in hard currency. However, people fight and die over territory.

From success to stress: China's claim on Taiwan is unwavering, but the old Nationalists have fortified the island. China's maritime advance eastward threatens Japan. China has claimed other islands in the East China Sea.

Chapter Abbreviation Key

A2/AD = Anti-access, area denial

BRI, OBOR = Belt and Road Initiative, One Belt One Road; two names for the same strategic project

CCP = Chinese Communist Party

EEZ = Exclusive economic zone

FONOP = US acronym for Freedom of navigation operation

PLA, PLAN, PLAAF = People's Liberation Army, People's Liberation Army Navy, People's Liberation Army Air Force

PRC = People's Republic of China

SCS = South China Sea

SLOC = Sea lines of communication

SOEs = Chinese state-owned enterprises (many are relics of Mao Tse-Tungs's Communist economic policies)

UNCLOS = United Nations Convention on the Law of the Sea

Expanding Chinese power exerted on the land axis (Silk Road Belt) could lead to another war with India, the war of Asia's giants.

As for the southern maritime advance: Clashes in the SCS over islands and fishing rights occurred in the 1970s, but serious Chinese territorial expansion operations on the southern sea axis began in the early 1990s. (See the Introduction.)

China has tried to diplomatically frame the SCS as a petty, bilateral struggle over islets and reefs between China and upstart neighbors. The SCS maritime zone, however, has global import—pun intended. An estimated five trillion dollars per year in trade (goods and resources) transits the SCS.

By disregarding fundamental international law and building artificial islands in international water, China's territory-grabbing SCS advance has set diplomatic, military, and legal conditions for a regional war and perhaps global war with the US Beijing's South China Sea gambit is a calculated imperial invasion that has become a strategic meeting engagement with America—a dangerous cocktail from hell indeed.

Overview: Twenty-First-Century China's Great Dilemma

When Deng Xiaoping became China's head of state, he promoted "socialism with Chinese characteristics." To prosper, China needed "freer" markets for agriculture and industry. Prosperity would permit the acquisition of modern technology and provide the cash to transform the military. China must modernize in key sectors: agriculture, industry, defense, and science and technology. Deng called these the Four Modernizations. Deng's modernizations had subtle but politically powerful roots. At the 1975 National People's Congress, Premier Chou Enlai, Mao Tse-Tung's great lieutenant, had publicly stated China must undertake comprehensive modernization.

In 1978, Deng articulated his policy guidance for modernization: "one center, two basic points." Economic development was the central focus (one center), but China would adhere to what he called opening-up and reform guidelines while maintaining Communist Party control. In 1979, he articulated the Four Cardinal Principles, which doctrinally enshrined strict CCP authoritarianism: China must "uphold" the socialist path, support the "democratic" dictatorship, follow CCP leadership, and follow Mao's thought.

Opening-up and reform policies would create a market economy within the socialist state, promote global economic links, and give China access to international markets. Deng argued a planned economy and a market economy could both exist within an authoritarian socialist system.

Hence China's twenty-first-century great dilemma: the Four Cardinal Principles fundamentally oppose the free-market energy, economic experimentation, and information connectivity that opening up and reform leverages to prime and sustain economic growth. Deng's reformist economic policies contradicted his restrictive ideology.

In the twenty-first century, China confronts this dichotomy twenty-four hours a day. The government wants foreign investment in China's economy while simultaneously discouraging direct participation that might challenge CCP authority. The tension between party authority and free-market mechanisms is why the CCP attempts to "guide" public opinion (exert narrative control), crush dissent, and resist demands that it share governmental power.

Riding The Tiananmen Tiger

The Great Dilemma has led to spilled blood in the twentieth century. In 1989, China's economic reforms were giving the people a taste of prosperity. In Beijing's Tiananmen Square, the CCP heard free-market-spurred calls for political reform. One group made a foam and papier-mâché statue it called the *Goddess of Democracy*.

Deng ordered People's Liberation Army tanks to attack the demonstrators. The PLA complied and killed at least two thousand people. Some sources contend the death toll was much higher.

Tiananmen is still a lurking tiger.

Since Tiananmen, the government has taken what several commentators call a gradualist approach to reform while stiffening penalties for dissent. However, in 2011, as the Arab Spring erupted in the Middle East, media reported that over the preceding five years, about one hundred thousand protests a year had occurred in China. Various issues provoked these public demonstrations of discontent, including forced relocation (for example, the Three Gorges Dam project), corruption in government officials, and environmental pollution.

Naval Modernization Contributes to Economic Security

Deng concluded that protecting Chinese national and economic security in the interdependent international system meant that China had to become a naval power as well as a land power. A potent, modern navy could protect Chinese sovereignty and its economy's international connections. As a first step, China's navy had to be able to deny a more powerful naval enemy access to the immediate area or make entering it extremely costly—anti-access, area denial (A2/AD) in military lingo. Eventually, a large Chinese navy would be able to protect international shipping lanes connecting China to energy supplies and other natural resources.

South China Sea Adventures: A Short History

China's expanding maritime capabilities empower its bid to secure control of the South China Sea's vital sea lanes and assert sovereignty over what it (speciously) claims is lost Chinese territory. Exploration geologists have evidence that the SCS seabed has large oil and gas deposits—a resource bonus!

As the twenty-first century's second decade ends and its third begins, in the South China Sea political power grows out of Chinese gun barrels and barrel upon barrel of Chinese concrete. Since the late 1990s, China has been expanding its bases in the Paracel Islands. It has also constructed artificial islands in the sea, particularly amid the Spratly Islands, and topped them with runways capable of handling strike aircraft. Chinese naval and air forces are capable of fighting an anti-access campaign and are able to project power. In 2012, Beijing attempted to diplomatically and legally project power when it claimed control of eighty-five percent of the SCS' nearly 2.2 million square miles. The jaw-dropping Nine-Dash Line demarcating China's claim dips south hundreds of miles from China's coast to near the island of Borneo, encroaching on territory belonging to the Philippines, Vietnam, Malaysia, and Brunei. In 2016, the Hague's international arbitration tribunal supported the Philippines' accusation that China had intruded on Filipino territory by seizing sea features and islets and conducting illegal fishing operations. China ignored the verdict.

The tribunal relied heavily on the UN Convention on the Law of the Sea treaty. UNCLOS has done many things, including codifying the geo-physical conditions and legal precedents that establish sovereign control of territorial waters and sovereign rights in EEZs. The Philippines disputed China's claim to Scarborough Shoal in the Spratlys. In 2012, Scarborough Shoal was a reef, a "sea feature" well inside long-recognized Filipino territory. The shoal is about 155 miles from the large inhabited Filipino island of Palawan. It is about 750 miles from China. Chinese construction barges anchored around the shoal, poured concrete, and created an island.

China has repeated this operation, leveraging military, economic, and information assets, economic sticks and carrots, and military and diplomatic intimidation to conduct a slow, steady imperialist invasion of the SCS. The process is quite a potent cocktail when applied to a weaker adversary. China's invasion has employed a variety of weapons, such as offshore construction barges, construction crews, and exploratory oil-drilling rigs, all supported by shepherding coast guard vessels and swarms of fishing boats. Construction task forces (economic assets) protected by military or paramilitary forces (military) create physical facts. Using dredges and lots of concrete, a construction task force turns what geographers call features (rocks, shoals, and the like) into man-made islands. The task force then tops its manufactured islet with military-grade runways capable of handling high-performance combat aircraft. If the final product looks something like a stationary naval aircraft carrier surrounded by a strip of sand, that isn't a glitch, it's a feature (additional military power). China then claims sovereignty (diplomatic and legal warfare) and vehemently argues (information and narrative warfare) that foreign ships need permission (legal warfare) to enter the "territorial waters" of these fakes. Chinese diplomats, scholars, lawyers, and media then defend the legitimacy of Beijing's concrete concoctions as if they were defending China's claim to central Beijing (more narrative and legal warfare).

In May 2014, China and Vietnam squared off over a Chinese oil-drilling project in Vietnamese waters. Vietnam saw the expedition as another step toward extending Chinese sovereignty to the Nine-Dash Line. The May 2014 clash had no fatalities, but other clashes spilled blood, such as the 1992 Da Luc Reef incident mentioned in the Introduction.

Key Actors, Their Goals and Risks
China

Goal: Maintain its territorial integrity and assume sovereign control over what it considers to be lost territories. China once again controls Hong Kong and Macau. But not Taiwan.

Goal: Protect and strengthen China's domestic economy and promote and protect China's foreign economic interests. Economic success is a source of national pride. The Chinese people are proud of their economic achievements.

Risk: India dominates China's sea lines of communication (SLOCs) through the Indian Ocean. China has begun to project naval power into the Indian Ocean. It has a base in Djibouti. It is developing facilities in Pakistan (Gawdar).

Risk: China publicly says that using military forces to invade Taiwan is a viable and justified option.

Risk: Communism is not ideologically attractive. Nationalism, powered by successful expansion, might be a substitute. So might an authoritarian revival narrative. (See the Known 6.)

United States

Goal: Asia matters to America. Since WWII, the US has invested enormous human, political, economic, technological, and military capital in Asia. Japan and South Korea were wildly successful American endeavors. In 1950, both nations were wrecks; today, they are wealthy democracies. America did fail in Vietnam. South Vietnam lost the Vietnam War, but Vietnam (North Vietnam) now needs a US ally. For the nations in East Asia, the United States remains the only power capable of penalizing Chinese misbehavior and encouraging good behavior.

Goal: The US is a fervent advocate of freedom of navigation. China's SCS shenanigans restrict freedom of navigation.

Frustrated Goal: As China modernized, the US bet that political liberalization would follow. International integration would mellow and moderate China's Communists. It didn't happen.

Risk: The US seeks to prevent the rise of a regional hegemon in East Asia, and East and Southeast Asian supremacy seems to be China's goal.

Narrative-Diplomatic Cocktail Message to Beijing and New Delhi, with a Military Twist: The US Has Renamed Its Military Pacific Command (PACOM) the Indo-Pacific Command (USINDOPACOM).

India

Since China's 1950 invasion of Tibet, India and China have had a difficult security relationship. Yet India and China can and do cooperate. Bilateral trade between the giants is over seventy billion dollars a year.

Goals: India wants to modernize its economy, secure its territory, and secure its interests.

Risk: Nuclear-armed Pakistan is nuclear-armed India's primary nemesis, and nuclear-armed China has served as Pakistan's most consistent ally.

Emerging Risks: China and India have armed confrontations over disputed territory in the Himalayas. China is acquiring bases in the Indian Ocean. Its new seaport facility in Gwadar, Pakistan and its new base in Djibouti worry India. So do Chinese intrigues in Indian Ocean nations such as the Maldives.

Possible Strategic Policy Adjustment: These and other Chinese power projection operations have led India to seriously reconsider its longstanding policies of non-alignment and "strategic autonomy"; India's participation in the Quad (see the following sub-section) is an indicator.

Japan

The Japanese know the Chinese despise them. They despise the Chinese. (See chapter two's discussion of East Asian ethnic animosity.)

Goal: Japan wants to avoid escalating boundary disputes with China. It seeks stability.

Risk: China insists that its maritime boundaries include the resource-rich East China Sea islets that Japan calls the Senkakus and China calls the Diaoyus. Japan is not about to let China seize control of its islands or encroach on its territorial prerogatives (see Known 8, following, the ADIZ nudge). Japan has offered to negotiate mutual development deals with China in waters around the Senkakus. Should China reject that diplomatic-economic cocktail, Japan's capable naval and air forces can give China a taste of A2/AD in the East China Sea, especially with US support.

The Quad

The Quadrilateral Security Dialogue (QSD) is a semi-official coalition with the United States, Japan, India, and Australia as its members. These nations regard China as a disruptive actor in what they now call the Indo-Pacific region. The Quad held its informal first meeting in 2007. Quad nations hold naval exercises and sometimes include a quint, Singapore.

Vietnam and the Philippines

Shared Manila–Hanoi Narrative, Supported By International Law: China has stolen their territory and plundered their resources.

Goal: Build security relationships that discourage further territorial encroachment. An alliance with the US is extremely valuable and the Philippines has one. Vietnam and India may expand their defense relationship. Indian naval vessels visiting in Vietnamese ports send a message.

Goal: To combat China, both nations are developing their own version of A2/AD naval and air forces. Vietnam intends to position advanced anti-ship missiles on its islands and along its coastline.

Diplomatic Ambiguity: The current Filipino government has downplayed The Hague tribunal's favorable UNCLOS ruling, which at the time indicated a willingness to reach an accommodation. However, words are not deeds. The Philippines is also engaged in an extensive military modernization program.

Taiwan

Beijing vows to recover "the lost province." Despite China's improved military capabilities, recent elections indicate the Taiwanese prefer independence. Tiananmen Square and China's failure to respect its promises to protect Hong Kong's democratic freedoms have given the Taiwanese added spine. Taiwan's Chinese understand that China is pursuing a very Chinese strategy of avoiding battle while attempting to wear down a weaker opponent economically and morally.

Singapore

The island city-state on the Strait of Malacca sees the slow advance of the artificial islands. They are heading south. The Strait is one of the planet's busiest seaways, an international economic funnel connecting the Pacific and Indian Oceans—which means it is a high-value military and economic choke point.

ASEAN

The Association of Southeast Asian Nations consists of Brunei, Cambodia, Indonesia, Laos, Malaysia, Myanmar, Philippines, Singapore, Thailand, and Vietnam. Each nation has a stake in the South China Sea.

Nine Knowns

Known 1: Chinese military modernization is in high gear. China is acquiring advanced nuclear submarines and aircraft carriers. How much China spends on defense is a subject of intense interest and debate. In 2010, the Pentagon estimated that China's military budget was about one hundred and fifty billion dollars a year. Other sources said one hundred billion dollars. Common estimates for 2015 were two percent of its GDP—around two hundred and ten billion dollars.

Known 2: China's PLA is a "party" army. It serves the party vanguard, not the Chinese people. (See Riding The Tiananmen Tiger in this chapter.)

Known 3: The Chinese military calls outer space a vital security domain, meaning it is a war zone. China is developing an active defense policy for space analogous to the naval active defense policy Deng deemed necessary in the late 1970s. In 2015, the Chinese government published a study attempting to unify Chinese strategy in order to win "informationized local wars"—Beijing's term for multi-domain cocktail warfare. The study argued cyber space and outer space have become "command posts" and recommended the PLAN shift from offshore-waters defense to a strategy combining offshore-waters defense and open-seas protection, which is mil-speak for blue water operations that can project power and protect commerce.

Known 4: Russia has never returned any Chinese territory seized by the czars in the nineteenth century, though in 1917, the Bolsheviks acknowledged that czarist treaties forced on China were coercive and predatory.

Known 5: In July 2009, riots pitting ethnic Han Chinese against ethnic (Turkic) Uighurs erupted in China's western Xinjiang Province. At least 180 people died; one thousand were injured. Chinese police and paramilitary forces arrested fifteen hundred. The Uighurs oppose the government's "Sinicization policy," which settles ethnic Han in the province. Though officially designated the Xinjiang Uighur Autonomous Region, the region is not autonomous and, as time passes, is becoming less Uighur.

Known 6: China's "century of humiliation" narrative has definite political traction within China. That narrative says imperialist powers from 1840 to 1949 bullied and robbed China. It then adds China's strong twenty-first century government won't let it happen again. What constitutes a strong Chinese government? Several narratives have emerged. Most of them contend a strong government recovers lost territory. A dedicated caste of Chinese academics and philosophes has fabricated an ideological alternative to what they call the US-led "liberal international order" (a term with its own abbreviation, LIO). The dedicated academics and philosophers portray China's dictatorship as a successful ideological competitor to the LIO. China's authoritarian governance model works (the Four Cardinal Principles), and China's economic success proves it works. However, upon close scrutiny problems emerge. Close scrutiny exposes the LIO as an ambiguous, strawman-esque concept, akin to twentieth-century Soviet propaganda describing the evils of democracy and free enterprise. In other words, Beijing's high brows are plagiarizing Cold War Communist propaganda.

Known 7: Chinese military analysts relentlessly discuss extending China's reach beyond the first island chain (which is roughly Japan, Taiwan, and the South China Sea) to the second (a wide arc running from Singapore through Guam and then north to Japan). Japan, Australia, and the US pay attention to this discussion, for in blunt language, reaching the second island chain translates as: "US Navy, go farther away."

Known 8: In November 2013, China tested Japanese and South Korean political and military reactions by extending its Air Defense Identification Zone (ADIZ) over contested islets and maritime boundaries. Tensions spiked as Tokyo and Seoul threatened retaliation. The ADIZ ploy had immediate consequences and strategic implications. Aircraft entering a recognized ADIZ must identify themselves to the national air controllers managing it. Should they fail to do so, they risk interception. Japan was the primary strategic target of China's ADIZ nudge. The new zone grabbed airspace above the disputed Senkaku/Diaoyu islets. The nudge also included a South Korean reef. China doesn't nudge for fishing rights; it was testing US reactions. America reacted: two unarmed USAF B-52s flew through the new zone, from Guam to South Korea. China has pulled a similar stunt in the South China Sea, demanding that passing aircraft recognize Chinese authority over fake island airspace.

Known 9: For years, China has sought to divide and conquer in the South China Sea. China insists on settling disputes bilaterally—meaning it intends to isolate and bully its weaker Southeast Asian neighbors.

Five Unknowns

Unknown 1: Has China identified its strategic opponent? Qiao and Wang suggest it has: the US.

Unknown 2: Is China strategically "locked in" on its SCS territorial grab or does the CCP dictatorship have room for a strategic course correction? If China cannot moderate its territorial demands, the chance of a military clash with the US increases dramatically.

Unknown 3: China has a long history of internal regional friction. Beijing confronts a dramatic imbalance in regional development. The east coast is bucks-up rich, the central provinces lag, and the western provinces are far behind. Regional differences in economic growth within China increase the possibility of conflict along regional lines. Regional warlords plagued China in the nineteenth and twentieth centuries. Other potential sources of domestic unrest worry Beijing. The *liudong renkou* ("floating population") problem occurs in urban areas throughout China. At any given time, some one hundred million people are away from their hometowns seeking work.

Unknown 4: Related to Unknown 3. Has China's economic and political rise plateaued? This is a frequent subject of foreign policy speculation in Asia and the West and "plateaued" is the preferred verb. Here is one thread of the discussion: the dictatorship must continue to purchase its legitimacy through economic reward and increasing wealth. If it fails to do so, The Tiananmen Tiger bares its fangs. An economic plateau is not an economic collapse; however, diminished economic expectations might result in less civic cooperation. Few economists foresee a Chinese economic bust in the next fifteen years, but economic slowdowns are inevitable.

Unknown 5: Has China fundamentally changed its political relationship with North Korea? (See chapter two.)

Relevant History and Geography

The early nineteenth century found the great Chinese empire technologically weak and politically fossilized. Foreign powers took advantage and seized slices of prime territory. The First Opium War, between China and Great Britain, was a notorious example. The Treaty of Nanking (1842) ended the war but forced China to give Britain sovereign control of the port of Hong Kong. Other European Great Power interventions followed. They forced China to cede territory, accept unfair trade agreements, and establish treaty ports—special zones in Chinese seaports where foreign powers exercised authority.

Internal turmoil also afflicted China with the Taiping Rebellion (1850–1864) a very fatal example. Thirty million people died in that spasm of anarchy. The crippled emperor clung to power. The twentieth century's first decade found the emperor a figurehead and his empire divided among warlords. The last emperor abdicated in 1911. Regional warlords fought among themselves and made deals with foreign powers.

On September 19, 1931, the morning after what became known as the Mukden Incident, Japanese soldiers attacked the Chinese garrison at Mukden (Shenyang) and invaded Manchuria. Some historians call it the first battle of World War II.

World War II utterly savaged China. In 1945, the Nationalists under Chiang Kai-shek and the Communists under Mao Tse-Tung continued their civil war until the Nationalists' defeat in 1949.

In 1950, China intervened in North Korea (see chapter two) and invaded Tibet. The Communists defended their action by claiming that traditionally Tibet belonged to China. As progressive Communists, they argued they were liberating Tibet from non-progressive Buddhist zealots. Invading Tibet took two weeks. By mid-1951, Beijing had full control of the country and annexed it.

In Indochina, China supported the Communist Viet Minh's post-World War II insurgency against France. The Viet Minh became North Vietnam. China supported North Vietnam in its war against South Vietnam and the US; South Vietnam lost.

In 1959, India gave Tibet's Dalai Lama refuge. An affronted Mao saw India as a threat to China's interests. China and India also had two serious border disputes in the Himalayas (which remain unresolved.) At the time, both Asian giants were developing nations with huge infantry armies. In 1962, China launched the Sino-Indian War and attacked India in the two disputed sectors. China's offensive began during the Cuban Missile Crisis. As the world focused on the US-Soviet Union confrontation, Beijing used bayonets to define the Himalayan border. (See the Introduction and the timing of China's island seizure in 1992.) Chinese forces, acclimated to the high altitudes, quickly defeated the Indian soldiers who rushed north to stop the offensive. The defeat still rankles the Indian Army.

* * * * *

In 1975, China had nine hundred million people, a central geographic position in East Asia, a land army with millions of troops, and nuclear weapons—definitely enormous power, but of a limited, defensive type.

War and Communist zealotry had exhausted the country. Mao's self-inflicted terror, the Great Cultural Revolution (1966–1976), wouldn't end for another year. Mao started the revolution with the stated goal of creating a socialist utopia. Ten million people died during his terror.

In 1979, the Sino–Vietnamese War erupted when China launched an attack to "teach Vietnam a lesson." The battle-hardened Vietnamese Army dealt the Chinese a bitter defeat. China disputes claims that it lost twenty-thousand soldiers in the month-long campaign. The war exposed Chinese military inadequacies and ensured that key members of China's military leadership supported the economic and technical modernization programs.

China's Geographic Neighborhood

China's legal border touches fourteen other countries. Clockwise from the south: Vietnam, Laos, Burma, Bhutan, Nepal, India, Pakistan, Afghanistan, Tajikistan, Kyrgyzstan, Kazakhstan, Mongolia, Russia, North Korea, Vietnam, and Laos.

South China Sea Territorial Claims (Diplomatic, Narrative, and Legal Operations)

Vietnam, Taiwan, and China claim islands in the Paracel archipelago. The Spratlys dot about seventy-thousand square miles of ocean area. China, Vietnam, and Taiwan claim the Spratlys in their entirety. The Philippines, Malaysia, and Brunei claim part of the Spratly archipelago.

Both island chains are located beyond the geological continental shelf of South China Sea states.

China, citing Han Dynasty references from the second century BC, claims its seamen first explored and named the Paracels; China's claims are legally suspect. Vietnam bases its claims on seventeenth, eighteenth, and nineteenth-century documents and maps. A Dutch East India Company document dated 1634 reported that the Vietnamese controlled the Paracels.

Two China-India Border Disputes

Border incidents occur with regularity along the twenty-five hundred mile border between China and India.

The most dangerous clashes occur in two places where the borders are disputed. In the east, Chinese and Indian military forces clash near the "trijunction" of the India-Bhutan-China border. Prior to 1950, the area was the trijunction of the India-Bhutan-Tibet border. The Doklam plateau is a hotspot. India believes China wants to seize the Sikkim and Siliguri Corridors. (Siliguri is a major city in India's West Bengal state, and is "the gateway" to northeast India.) In June 2017, an Indian Army patrol disrupted a Chinese construction crew building a road along the disputed Tibet–Bhutan border.

In the west, China and India spar over the Line of Actual Control in the Karakoram sector, near the junction of the China-Pakistan-India border and along the northern edge of Kashmir province. The Line of Actual Control stretches from Arunachal Pradesh to Aksai

Chin. China claims both areas and occupies Aksai Chin. Pakistan ceded its slice of Aksai Chin to China in 1963.

Early 2018: China has a superior road network leading to its positions in the disputed regions. The road network gives China superior supply capabilities and the ability to quickly reinforce deployed units. China reportedly sees India's improved small forward airfields in the Karakoram sector as a signal that India intends to improve its ability to reinforce that disputed zone. India contends that China's Himalayan cocktail of military preparations, diplomacy, narrative operations and the BRI is similar to the aggressive cocktails it employs in the East and South China Seas.

Operational and Strategic Complexities to Ponder

Complexity 1: China's estimated population in 2017 was 1.4 billion. Ninety-one percent of its people are ethnic Han Chinese. Nine percent are ethnic minorities—but that is still one hundred thirty-nine million people. China's Han population is also rapidly aging. The one-child policy imposed by the CCP on ethnic Han families from 1979 to 2016 contributed to this demographic issue. With exceptions, the policy imposed a one-child-per-family limit. China's dictatorship believed the country faced an overpopulation problem; however, Beijing failed to understand "overpopulation" is a wicked problem with hazy variables. China could face a worker shortage in the 2020s and 2030s.

Complexity 2: In May 2013, a Chinese general boasted China would secure its South China Sea territorial claims by wrapping them with ships, air patrols, and garrisons, the military "layers" akin to protective cabbage leaves. At the time, military cabbage was sprouting around Scarborough Shoal in Filipino waters. China's artificial islands now have air and naval bases. China's cabbage strategy includes Chinese maritime gray-zone operations that employ civilian cabbage: construction barges, drilling rigs entering disputed waters, swarms of fishing boats fishing in disputed waters, and Coast Guard ships conducting patrols in disputed zones. China is using the same tactics in other maritime disputes.

Complexity 3: China has declined to explain how its SCS claims align with UNCLOS requirements. For the most part, they don't; they flout law and international agreements. In 2002, Beijing signed a joint declaration with ASEAN in which the parties agreed to exercise self-restraint in the South China Sea and refrain from occupying uninhabited features. Between 2009 and 2017, Chinese construction crews turned seven uninhabitable sea features (rocks and reefs submerged at high tide) into artificial islands.

Select Actor Cocktails

China

Narratives: China insists that its growing military power is defensive. Beijing delivers its narratives via the usual methods, but one of the more interesting is its Confucius Institutes. The institutes are a project of Hanban, an agency under the Chinese Ministry of Education. Hanban controls the institutes. They attempt to influence the approximately seventy million Chinese living overseas, with Chinese university students a specific target audience. Confucius Institutes are genuine diplomatic and information warfare instruments. The institutes avoid discussion of forbidden topics like the Tiananmen Square massacre.

Military-Information Operation: In the South China Sea, China now conducts combined patrols with aircraft and naval vessels. These patrols may include long-range bombers flying from bases on China's coast. These are show-of-force operations as well as patrols. China is demonstrating that its military has the ability to conduct combat operations 900–1200 miles from its coastline.

Camouflaged in Silk: The BRI as a Multi-Decade Diplomatic, Economic, Narrative, and Military Operation

In 2013, President Xi Jinping announced China would sponsor a multi-decade international commercial and infrastructure development project. The Belt and Road Initiative would be a twenty-first century version of the ancient Silk Road that ran west from China through Central Asia—that's the information narrative. The project would have land and maritime components: The Silk Road Economic Belt (land) and the twenty-first century Maritime Silk Road (sea). Beijing guarantees all BRI participants will prosper.

The land component, "the Belt," consists of highways, railroads, pipelines, and other infrastructure projects (power generation and power grid) built within a very broad Central Asian corridor and connecting to Europe, Southwest Asia, and the eastern Mediterranean littoral. The Maritime Silk Road links China by sea to Africa and southwest Asia and, via the Suez Canal, to Europe. On the BRI's sea leg, China will help build seaports, improve old ports and port facilities, and improve the ports' regional land transportation infrastructure.

Beijing plans to complete the BRI by 2049, the one-hundredth anniversary of Communist rule in China.

How much will the BRI cost? No one knows; two to three trillion dollars is a rumored estimate. The three-trillion figure may not include Chinese state subsidies.

China promises to invest in nations that participate in Belt land and Road sea projects. What developing country could turn down this no-strings-attached offer?

The answer: countries that know an economic hook when one is dangled.

Add military power to the BRI cocktail. Highways, railroads, and seaports serve commercial purposes—like shipping silk—but they are also military assets. Military planners worldwide point out China could use improved highway and rail links in Central Asia to quickly deploy Chinese military forces to places like Pakistan. The Central Asian highways and railroads circumvent the Strait of Malacca chokepoint.

India sees benefit in some projects and has signed a BRI Memorandum of Understanding with China. However, savvy Indian defense officials see one Chinese Road project as a threat: the deep-water port of Gawdar in Pakistan's Baluchistan province (which borders Iran). China is building a huge navy. Its artificial island invasion is approaching the Strait of Malacca. Gawdar is a perfect base for Chinese blue water fleet—an Indian Ocean Chinese base challenging the Indian Navy.

Many BRI projects are expensive and not economically viable for private construction firms, so they are built by Chinese state-owned enterprises (SOEs). As of 2018, Chinese SOEs have the BRI's largest construction contracts. Reportedly, Chinese SOEs try to take an ownership interest in their projects. When they do, Beijing has long-term influence. Investment becomes a potential weapon. Does this indicate the economic development chatter and Silk Road infrastructure is camouflage—or cabbage—for securing Chinese military objectives?

The BRI could easily create a situation that nineteenth-century British imperialists would recognize: should China insist on providing Chinese "security assistance units" to protect construction operations in dangerous areas, what happens when countries in the vicinity determine the Chinese forces threaten them? Maritime Silk Road? China's illegal artificial island-building campaign in the South China Sea is a maritime development project that has encroached on other nations' sovereignty.

Given their geographic, cultural, political, and engineering challenges, some BRI mega-projects could become mega-economic and political disasters that drain Beijing financially and diplomatically.

United States

Military and Diplomatic Initiatives in the SCS: The US is confirming its commitment to its alliances and partners and demonstrating its commitment to freedom of the seas. The US intends to build a network of states dedicated to free markets in Asia. It will maintain ties with Taiwan in accordance with its increasingly elastic interpretation of the "One-China" policy.

Freedom of Navigation Operations (FONOPs)— US Navy Diplomatic, Military, Economic, and Information Cocktail

The U.S. Navy and State Department take pains to distinguish a FONOP from routine naval operations and routine freedom of navigation.

A FONOP takes place in the SCS when a US Navy vessel sails close to a disputed feature occupied (created) by China. During a FONOP, a warship must conduct a simple military drill. Drills may not be conducted during an innocent passage. The drill indicates that the ship is exercising high-seas freedoms near the disputed sea feature.

An American Narrative Shift: America's optimism regarding China's future has turned to pushback pessimism. The militarization of the South China Sea and the frequent demonization of the US by Chinese military leaders have soured the US-China relationship. The US now demands trade concessions from China.

India

India is modernizing its military forces and enlarging its navy. India's participation in the Quad worries China, and India wants China to worry about its participation in the Quad. The Quad is a powerful anti-Chinese diplomatic, military, and economic cocktail. India forces China to defend another front. (See the following War of the Quad.)

Diplomatic and Military Scenarios

This list is meant to be illustrative; it is not complete. These scenarios are speculations, not predictions.

1. **Meeting Engagement in the South China Sea.** A sea battle sparks a short but deadly war between the US and China in the SCS with the Philippines and Vietnam likely US allies. Here's an example of a triggering event: Chinese and Filipino vessels exchange fire, the US Navy attempts to intervene, and a Chinese missile hits a USN warship. Another trigger: A Chinese decision

to militarily restrict the passage of freighters and tankers in transit to Taiwan or Japan could bring a US embargo-busting response. Both scenarios could lead to a wide-ranging air and sea war along the entire East Asian littoral—in others words, a devastating regional war that produces a global economic recession.

2. **China Invades Taiwan.** China launches an amphibious assault on Taiwan. The attack might start with a "missile drizzle," with thousands of short- and medium-range missiles and smart weapons slowly eroding Taiwanese defenses. China might try a surprise attack using air-cushion vehicles, helicopters, and paratroopers to quickly insert infantry forces. This attack would likely ignite a major war with the US.

3. **The A2/AD War.** A US fleet including stealth aircraft and "dispersed fire platforms" leaves the central or south Pacific and approaches the Chinese coast. China responds with long-range "warning fires." One of the warning shots strikes and sinks an American ship. The US fleet responds with long-range warning fires of its own. Major air bases in southern China are destroyed. Every SCS artificial islet is pulverized. American smart mines seal every major Chinese seaport. (This scenario illustrates capabilities that already exist.)

4. **China versus India.** Call this the Sino-Indian War, Round Two, or the War for Southern Tibet. Likely scenario: China launches a limited invasion with the goal pushing the border twenty-five to thirty miles farther south in both the eastern and western sectors. China would quickly call for a ceasefire to avoid escalation to nuclear war and offer to negotiate a permanent border demarcation.

5. **War of the Quad.** Versions of scenarios one and three could occur that have India, Australia, Japan, and the US conducting combat operations against China. In many respects this is Beijing's nightmare, for Vietnam could ally with the Quad. With India in action, China might urge Pakistan to launch conventional attacks on India or threaten India with nuclear attack. India might hit Pakistan with a pre-emptive nuclear strike. Outlandish? Let's hope so.

6. **The Next Chinese Revolution.** China reaches a domestic tipping point in, say, 2035. For a variety of reasons sketched or implied in this chapter—economic slowdown, ethnic unrest, loss of citizen cooperation, complete disgust with corruption—authoritarian control cannot be sustained. The Tiananmen Tiger bites back.

CHAPTER 4

TWENTY-FIRST CENTURY
RUSSIAN IMPERIAL WARFARE

According to the Kremlin, the Kosovo precedent justifies the Crimean precedent. A 2017 Balkan diplomatic dispute demonstrated Kosovo 1999's historical link to Crimea 2014. In January 2017, Kosovo accused neighboring Serbia of preparing to emulate "the Crimea model" and annex a predominantly ethnic Serb enclave within Kosovo and adjacent to the Serbian border. The accusation stirred fears of a rekindled Kosovo War (March 1998–June 1999). "The Crimea model" refers to the 2014 Russian invasion and annexation of Ukraine's Crimean peninsula and subsequent invasion of eastern Ukraine.

Overview

What does Russia want? What do Russians leaders want? Do they want money, a revived Russian empire, or both?

Chapter Abbreviation Key

ABM = Anti-ballistic missile (key U.S. systems are Patriot, THAAD,
Navy Aegis ABMs, and the ground-based interceptor GBI)

EFP = Enhanced Forward Presence (NATO military policy)

INF = Intermediate-range nuclear forces (INF). Major treaty signed
in 1988.

UAV = Unmanned aerial vehicle (drone)

UNSCR = United Nations Security Council Resolution

SSRs = Former Soviet Socialist republics (of the old Soviet Union, Union
of Soviet Socialist Republics, USSR)

RUBK = The author's acronym for a revived Russian empire consisting
of Russia, Ukraine, Belarus, and Kazakhstan

SALT = Strategic Arms Limitation Talks (1980s)

SVR = Russian Foreign Intelligence Service. The external intelligence
agency.

FSB = Russian internal intelligence service, the Federal Security Service

GRU = Main Intelligence Directorate. Russian military intelligence
service.

KOS = Russia's Special Operations Force Command (special forces
personnel)

SEZ = Special Economic Zone. The Kaliningrad Oblast is a Russian
Federation SEZ.

In their eras, czarist Russia and the Soviet Union were Great Powers. However, as the twenty-first century's third decade begins, Russia is an embittered remnant of the Cold War Soviet colossus.

Since the mid-1990s, the Kremlin's words and deeds have reflected deep resentment and anger spurred by Russia's loss of international stature. Those disturbing emotions were present in April 2005 when Russian president Vladimir Putin called the USSR's demise the "greatest geopolitical catastrophe of the [twentieth] century."

A revived empire and a productive economy are not mutually exclusive objectives. However, tensions exist that hinder their simultaneous pursuit. Building a strong, modernized military to revive the empire requires cash, so Russia needs a wealth-producing economy. However, corruption, bureaucratic inflexibility, and oligarchic self-interests hamper Russia's economy. Russia's authoritarian oligarchs fear the political reforms (especially rule-of-law reforms) that spur economic creativity. Russian armed aggression and episodic denial of natural gas supplies have made European countries wary trading partners.

The RUBK

Yet the Kremlin craves Great Power status.

The czarist and Soviet empires were largely self-sufficient entities possessing the people and resources to field powerful military forces. Russia has nuclear weapons, but when the USSR collapsed, the empire lost about half of its population.

What new imperial territorial configuration contains the resources to fully secure Great Power status for a revived Russia? The RUBK—pronounced "rubik," as in the puzzle Rubik's Cube—is one configuration. The RUBK consists of Russia, Ukraine, Belarus, and Kazakhstan. With its demographics and natural resources, the RUBK has the geo-strategic resources to secure global Great Power status.

The term RUBK appeared in a *Creators Syndicate* column I wrote in 2004. That column pinched a 1991 analysis that James F. Dunnigan and I conducted while writing the second edition of *A Quick and Dirty Guide to War*. Dunnigan and I concluded (before the USSR officially collapsed in December 1991) that the Russians would seek to retain or regain control of the core of their empire: Russia, Ukraine, Belarus, and Kazakhstan.

A quote from the 2004 column:

Super-power status takes money, and a large number of people (how large is arguable, but 200 million is a plausible figure). The common economic interests linking Russia, Ukraine, Belarus and Kazakhstan were a potential post-Cold War positive. Russia needed Ukraine's immense agricultural productivity. (Bay 2004)

That column added this thought:

"A democratic Ukraine could do for Russia what Poland did for Ukraine—provide a next-door, you-can-do-it-too example of the benefits of the rule of law and economic liberalization. Ultimately, another organization, the EU, provides more stability and prosperity than an antiquated, authoritarian and corrupt RUBK ever could."

In 2014, Russian leaders began using a new term, "New Russia" (*Novorossiya*), to describe their goals in Ukraine. The New Russia project included regaining control of nine regions of Ukraine.

In 2018, Russia wields immense political and economic influence in Kazakhstan. Belarus has avoided complete Kremlin political control, but the Russian Army routinely conducts war games in Belarus that often include offensive operations.

What does Belarus do if the Russian Army decides to stay?

The Kosovo and Ukraine Precedents

In March 1999, NATO military forces intervened in the Kosovo War with orders to stop Serb "ethnic cleansing" attacks on Kosovar Albanians. NATO said its military forces were armed peacekeepers deployed to enforce UN Security Council Resolution 1199, which demanded that Serb security forces in Kosovo terminate their genocidal campaign. NATO forces did not enter Kosovo to seize territory.

Russia bitterly opposed what it called an "illegal" foreign intervention. In Kosovo—sovereign Serbian territory—Belgrade waged legitimate war against insurgent ethnic separatists. The Kremlin accused NATO of invading Slavic Serbian territory. The ethnic Slav reference connected the Kremlin's 1999 Balkan diplomacy to Czarist Pan-Slavism. Imperial Russia claimed it had a mandate to protect Balkan Slavs—especially Orthodox Christian Slavs—from oppression by Turks, Germans, Austro-Hungarians, Italians, and sometimes the French and British. In 1999, Turkey, Germany, Italy, France, and Britain were NATO members. Hungary joined in March 1999. Many Serbs agreed with the Kremlin narrative.

The US Clinton administration, NATO, and the EU acknowledged the diplomatic complexities and assured Russia that the intervention was a one-off event to prevent a potential genocide akin to Bosnia 1992–1995 and Rwanda 1994.

NATO member Spain opposed the intervention. Worried about Basque and Catalan separatists, Madrid argued the intervention might encourage militant separatists worldwide, especially if Kosovo sought and secured independence from Serbia.

Russia refused to accept the one-off stipulation. According to the Kremlin's narrative, Kosovo established a precedent for foreign intervention to protect threatened ethnic factions.

In February 2008, Kosovo unilaterally declared independence.

In August 2008, the Russo-Georgia War began, with the Kremlin citing Kosovo as justification for invading Georgia.

Russia's 2008 invasion of Georgia employed an ancient imperialist offensive operation: the creeping war of aggression. The Kremlin used its Georgia offensive to experiment with creeping warfare fought under twenty-first century conditions. Russia conducted a propaganda campaign that portrayed its forces as peacekeepers protecting Abkhazia and South Ossetia from Georgian ethnic domination. During the war, Georgia was struck by cyber attacks that weren't directly traceable to the Russian government. Ukraine vigorously supported Georgia and harshly criticized Russia's military invasion and legal reasoning.

The Russo-Georgia War revived fears in Eastern Europe that Russia was expanding, attempting to revive and rebuild its empire.

To Poles, Balts, Bulgarians, Romanians, Moldovans, and definitely Ukrainians, Russia's 2014 seizure and annexation of Crimea confirmed the Kremlin's aggressive, revivalist goal. The Crimea caper shattered the 1994 Budapest Memorandum in which Russia guaranteed Ukrainian territorial sovereignty in exchange for Ukraine's nuclear weapons. That agreement helped stabilize post-Cold War Eastern Europe.

Kosovo became independent, but not Crimea. On March 18, 2014, the Kremlin annexed Crimea and made it Russian territory. For the first time since WWII, military aggression in Europe by a major power led to annexation and territorial expansion. The legacy of aggression, annexation, and expansion by a major European power is mass slaughter across the continent and, in the twentieth century, global war.

Russia's continuing war in eastern Ukraine directly targets Kiev, but dismantling NATO is also a goal. The Kremlin's incessant anti-NATO propaganda campaign confirms it. This is a typical pattern: Russian operatives and local proxies make false but sensational accusations such as "NATO is preparing to attack Russia" and

"NATO is militarizing the Black Sea." They repeat them, relentlessly, with anger and conviction. Digital media propagate the accusations, globally.

This narrative seeds suspicion and division. The Kremlin believes dividing NATO opens the whole of Eastern Europe to Russian domination.

Key Actors, Their Goals and Risks

Russia: The Nucleus of Russian Decision-Making

In the 1990s, members of the former USSR's Communist *nomenklatura*—government bosses and bureaucrats—used political cunning and intimidation to acquire the enterprises they managed during the Soviet era. Connected bureaucrats and former intelligence officers became involved in the *mafiya*, an emerging criminal class with international links and homicidal capability. From 1994 to 1996, over forty Russian bankers were murdered as *mafiya* organizations entered Russia's banking sector.

This malign combination of power, wealth, and criminal talent set the stage for what some commentators two decades ago called oligarchic power consolidation within Russia. The oligarchy operates beneath the veneer of free elections. (See chapter five for Iran's version.)

Though it has Soviet totalitarian origins, this oligarchy is not a totalitarian dictatorship. Since the late 1990s, Vladimir Putin has been a powerful member of the oligarchy's political and operational nucleus. Friendly billionaires, ex-KGB intelligence officers, and mafia with useful talents circle the nucleus. They are a new Russian royalty (*boyars*), with Putin being their "pop tsar."

Major Strategic Goal: Kremlin leaders are shamed by Russia's status as a "weak" Great Power. Russia must become a "complete" Great Power. Creating the RUBK is one way to achieve this goal. Russia already possesses nuclear forces.

Other Strategic Goals: Pry Turkey out of NATO. Neutralize Bulgaria and Romania. Neutralize or recover (occupy) NATO members Estonia, Latvia, and Lithuania.

Information-Political Goals Enhancing Domestic Prestige: The Russians coveted Crimea. As an act of Communist brotherhood, in 1954 then-Soviet premier Nikita Khrushchev gave Crimea to Ukraine. In 2014, twenty-three years after the Soviet Navy fragmented, Sevastopol, Crimea's major seaport, was still the Russian Navy's Black Sea Fleet's home port. The Kremlin also covets Ukraine. Kiev is regarded as the birthplace of the first Russian state, Kievan Rus. The site of one of Russia's greatest military victories, Poltava (1709), is in central Ukraine. At Poltava, Tsar Peter the Great defeated invading Swedes.

Military-Economic Operation: In 2017, credible Western military analysts estimated Russia had either updated or replaced half of its Cold War-era military equipment.

Military-Economic Vulnerability: Oil-price fluctuations affect Russian re-armament and military operations. Russian defense industries need export sales to generate cash to build high-tech weapons. When oil prices drop, this vulnerability becomes acute.

Operational Military Vulnerability: Digital media prevent the Kremlin from hiding the Russian casualties suffered in Ukraine—and for that matter, in Syria as well. Russian casualties have become a political liability for the oligarchy.

Information Warfare Operations in Ukraine: The Kremlin uses propaganda operations to blur its responsibility for tactical military attacks in Ukraine. The propaganda gambits confuse Western media attempting to cover Ukraine. The Kremlin also conducts local propaganda campaigns targeting Russian speakers in eastern Ukraine. One oft-repeated line fed to ethnic Russians in Ukraine: Ukrainian forces are "bloodthirsty thugs." This repeats 1975-era Soviet agitation propaganda, which described American forces in West Germany as gangsters and imperialist occupiers.

Possible Financial Operation to Vex EU/NATO Sanctions:

Should Western sanctions deny Russia Western financing, the Kremlin might turn to China.

Ukraine

Strategic Assessment of the Russian Invasion, March 2018: Kiev believes Russia's offensive has "stalemated." The Donbas frontline has shifted little since 2016. For Ukraine this is a limited success; it has survived over four years of creeping war, but there is little prospect that Kiev will recover its lost territory.

However, the episodic fighting and Russia's continued financial and military support for Eastern separatists has sapped Ukraine politically. The stalemate stymies economic growth and increases domestic debt.

Historic Risk: An East-West ethnic division splits Ukraine, and Russia exploits it. Eastern Ukraine borders Russia. During the Soviet era, many Russians settled in eastern Ukraine. During czarist times, the Russian Orthodox church held sway among faithful Eastern Ukrainian Slavs. Western Ukrainians tended to be Catholic, like their fellow Slavs to the west in Poland. Today, Western Ukrainians overwhelmingly favor European Union integration.

Operational Military Assessment, March 2018: Pro-Russian separatist forces have failed to take key Ukrainian cities (Mariupol, Slovyansk, and Lysychansk) along the frontline. To take them would require significant reinforcement with conventional Russian soldiers. That would increase Russian casualties.

Strategic Political Assessment of Ukraine: Though the Kremlin continues to exploit Ukraine's East-West ethnic divisions (Russians in the Donbas, Ukrainians in the west), the government believes that Russia's invasion has strengthened Ukrainian relations with NATO and the EU, making it less likely that Ukraine would accept any Russian peace offer demanding Ukrainian military and political neutrality.

Ukraine's Internal Corruption War (a Legal Operational Failure?): The Ukrainian government contends the invasion prevents it from effectively pursuing economic and political reform. Western creditors disagree. They have been disappointed with Ukraine's efforts to combat corruption.

Linked Diplomatic-Information-Economic Operations: Ukraine's parliament passed a law defining areas seized by pro-Russian separatists in the east as regions "temporarily occupied by Russia." In 2017 the government banned all trade with "occupied" Donetsk and Luhansk.

Diplomatic Operation Yields Military Cooperation: In 2016, NATO agreed to help train Ukrainian special operations forces. Ukraine had begun requesting the assistance in mid-2014.

NATO

Strategic Military and Diplomatic Deterrence: Article 5 of NATO's charter states that "an armed attack against one or more of them…shall be considered an attack against them all." If an aggressor attacks a member's territory or a member's forces, vessels, or aircraft operating in or over NATO territory, each member will take "action as it deems necessary, including the use of armed force, to restore and maintain" NATO security. Article 5 is occasionally referred to as "the Three Musketeers clause." The daring French musketeers promised one for all and all for one. Article 5 does as well. Article 5 is a diplomatic-military-information cocktail that contributed to winning the Cold War. It now protects former Warsaw Pact members Bulgaria, Romania, and Poland, and former SSRs Lithuania, Latvia, and Estonia.

Military-Information-Diplomatic Operation: NATO forces now routinely conduct military exercises in the Baltic states and in the territories of NATO members who formerly belonged to the Soviet Union's Warsaw Pact. The exercises are part of NATO's Enhanced Forward Presence (EFP) military program (reinforcing Eastern European members with NATO military forces from Western Europe and North America).

Denmark and Norway: Russian military provocations in the Baltics and in the Arctic Sea trouble NATO's Nordics. Russian aircraft carrying armed missiles have repeatedly bluffed attacks on the defenses of Denmark's Bornholm island, emulating Cold War-era probes. Denmark believes the probes are intended to weaken Danish support for Poland and Ukraine. Neutral Nordics Sweden and Finland have noticed. (See Unknown 2.)

In-Concert Diplomatic-Economic Operations: NATO now has twenty-nine members—that's a big committee, and each committee member has its own agenda. The March 2018 attempted assassination of a former Russian agent in Great Britain produced a NATO-wide diplomatic reaction. The British quickly tied the attack to the Kremlin. The would-be assassins used a banned chemical weapon in the attack. Britain characterized the attempt as a chemical warfare attack on its territory. In concert, Britain and British allies expelled Russian diplomats. The "in-concert" element is key. Stiff economic and political sanctions enforced in concert could do significant damage to Russia's economy.

Turkey: This NATO member is emerging as a political and military wildcard.

Poland: This NATO member provides Ukraine with material and moral support.

Operational Military Goal with Strategic Diplomatic Implications: In 2014, Polish officials recommended that NATO station two heavy (armored) brigades on Polish soil.

Military-Economic Operation: In 2015, Poland launched a thirty-six billion dollar defense modernization and expansion program.

NATO BALTIC States

Military-Diplomatic Operation with Strategic Diplomatic Implications: In May 2015, senior officials in the Baltic states asked the US to establish permanent military garrisons in their countries.

Cyber Operations: NATO has established a Cyber Defense Center in Estonia. In 2007, Estonia suffered sustained cyber attacks that did significant financial damage to the country. Estonia blamed Russia for the attacks.

United States

Strategic Economic and Diplomatic Operation: Thanks to the fracking revolution, the US has the power to affect (and often undercut) the price of global oil and natural gas. The sustained price plunge that began in 2013 has exposed the oligarchic Russian regime's strategic weakness: dependency on oil revenue.

Military-Diplomatic Operation: US anti-missile defenses are maturing. In May 2001, President Bush said the United States and the world needed a capable, limited missile defense system. The US missile shield is designed to protect NATO nations from "rogue state" attacks.

EU

The EU continues to support sanctions against Russia for annexing Crimea and waging war in the Donbas. It has also ratified a free-trade deal with Ukraine.

China

Strategic Economic Fact: China's GDP is more than seven times that of Russia. China is spending more than three times as much on defense as Russia.

Strategic Diplomatic and Economic Fact: China is now more of a Great Power than Russia.

Geo-Political Fact: Russia occupies Siberia (which China claims the czars stole). Can Russia defend it against Great Power China?

Secondary Actors

Non-Frontline Balkan States

Serbia remains a Russian ally.

As of early 2018, peacekeeping forces remain in Kosovo. A small EU-led peacekeeping contingent remains in Bosnia, with good reason. Bosnia's "split state," with Bosnian Muslims and Croats balancing Bosnian Serbs, just manages to creak along.

Wild Cards

Islamist Radicals in Former SSRs

Russia is waging counter-terror wars in the North Caucasus.

The Kremlin supports counterterrorism regimes in Dagestan and Chechnya. (See the introduction, Chechnya's insurgency persists.)

Mongolia: The Mongols want to be US allies.

Iran: A Russian ally in the economic war to maintain high oil prices. (See chapter five.)

Exploring the Russian Gray Zone

The Russo-Georgia War Preliminary

In August 2008, Russian forces invaded the nation of Georgia, igniting the Russo-Georgia War. The Kremlin used a creeping war of aggression to test Western will to defend the diplomatic agreements that stabilized post-Cold War Eastern Europe.

The 2008 invasion of Georgia employed military and political tactics similar to the ones Serbia used in its 1991 creeping war of aggression against Croatia.

The US government (the George W. Bush administration) met the Russian invasion with aggressive diplomatic action, seeking support from NATO allies and threatening Moscow with sanctions. It backed diplomacy with military action. As Russian Army regular units approached the Georgian capital, Tbilisi, the Georgian government asked the US to fly the Georgian Army brigade serving in Iraq home to Georgia. The US complied. Suddenly Russia confronted an additional twenty-five hundred well-trained and reasonably well-equipped Georgian soldiers.

The US airlift also gave Moscow pause. The airlift demonstrated Washington would act on behalf of an ally under attack.

In 2008, Putin was Russia's prime minister. He accused the US of orchestrating the war in order to benefit a presidential candidate, implicitly suggesting that Bush had started a war in Georgia in order to promote John McCain's candidacy.

The charge that America started the war was utterly false, but it continued the narrative theme that NATO was preparing to attack Russia.

On August 26, 2008, the Kremlin recognized South Ossetia and Abkhazia as independent states. The diplomatic move was a direct response to Kosovo's February 2008 declaration of independence.

In 2008, oil prices were comparatively high; Russia had money to spend on warfare. Restricted energy supplies enhanced Russian threats to curb natural gas shipments to Europe if the EU retaliated for the attack on Georgia by imposing economic sanctions.

Securing Russia's borders and protecting the interests of ethnic Russians are traditional Russian concerns. In 2008, protecting ethnic Russian communities in Georgia and Moldova's separatist statelet, Transdniestr, were Kremlin *causes célèbres*; in 2018 they still are.

Cocktail Warfare in Ukraine

In 2014, Russia did something it did not do in 2008: it seized and then annexed territory.

The annexation of Crimea continues to hinder productive negotiations with the Kremlin. Invading Ukrainian territory—much less annexing it—violated the Budapest Memorandum of 1994. The agreement guaranteed Ukraine's territorial integrity in exchange for Ukraine's de-nuclearization. Would Russia have attacked a Ukraine armed with nuclear weapons? We will never know.

Violating the memorandum challenged US and British guarantees regarding the defense of Eastern Europe. The US and Britain both signed the memorandum.

Ukraine Context of February 2014

The Russian invasion of Crimea followed several months of escalating "Euromaidan" protests in Kiev that led pro-Russian Ukrainian president Viktor Yanukovych to flee. Demonstrators claimed that pro-Yanukovych snipers in his security forces killed a hundred protestors.

The Kremlin's February 2014 invasion of Crimea updated the Russo-Georgia script. At the strategic level, Russia's "alliance" with the US in Syria gave the Kremlin a strategic lever to dampen a harsh reaction by the Obama administration. There were operational adaptations. In its initial stages (late February), Russian special operations personnel from KSO and elite infantry formations played a more obvious role in supporting "threatened ethnic Russians."

The March 2014 annexation of Crimea, however, was dedicated to the glory of reviving Russia, not humanitarian intervention. The day the Kremlin announced the annexation, Putin told an adoring crowd in Red Square, "We will do much more."

Invasion of Eastern Ukraine

In April 2014, Russian operatives and pro-Russian activists in eastern Ukraine launched another creeping war of aggression in eastern Ukraine. Moscow accused Ukrainians, Poles, and Americans of killing ethnic Russians. Anti-Russian ethnic violence was a prelude to an imminent ethnic-based civil war in eastern Ukraine. Given the dire life-or-death threat, the Kremlin had to take all necessary military and humanitarian actions to protect vulnerable ethnic Russians living in eastern Ukraine from violent attacks by Ukrainian fascists and ethnic fanatics.

Initial operations carved out rebel enclaves in the Donbas (Donets Basin).

In July 2014, a surface-to-air missile shot down Malaysia Airlines Flight 17 as it flew over eastern Ukraine. All 298 passengers aboard the flight died. Investigators concluded that Russian-backed separatists downed the commercial plane using a Russian-made missile. Moscow disputes this conclusion.

In August 2014, Russian tanks "flattened" the tiny Ukrainian border town of Novosvitlivka in a demonstration of Russian Army ground combat power. Ukraine reported that the tanks fired on every building in the town.

In fall 2014, however, a conflict pattern began to emerge in eastern Ukraine: Intense combat suddenly erupts. Russian-backed rebels—using Kremlin-supplied heavy artillery, mortars, and machine guns—launch a series of attacks on Ukrainian military positions. Other rebels raid neighborhoods or probe Ukrainian defenses, especially those around the Black Sea port of Mariupol.

Then the violence stops. All appears to be quiet on Europe's eastern front. Ukraine contends that Russian intelligence agents planned the attacks and Russian KSO officers directed them. The Kremlin denies supplying or financing the rebels and announces it has convinced the rebels to respect the ceasefire agreement with Ukraine. Russian propagandists promise peace, soothing the headline consciousness of US media. As a result, a war in Europe involving a nuclear power draws scant American attention.

The October 2016 surge in Donbas combat followed this script. After weeks of relative dormancy, international observers reported a surge in rebel violations of the Minsk ceasefire agreement. The rebels employed heavy weapons. By mid-November, defense analysts concluded that the number of rebel attacks launched in October was roughly twice the number launched in September.

The October surge occurred during a major media distraction: the hotly contested US presidential election.

* * * * *

This calculated cycle—a cocktail of kinetic military action, information warfare, and diplomatic subterfuge—guided Russia's creeping war of aggression in eastern Ukraine through spring 2018. A burst of planned, aggressive violence is followed by planned, well-propagandized dormancy. It is warfighting in twenty-first-century conditions.

Six Knowns

Known 1: Russia has built a bridge across the Kerch Strait and connected the Russian Federation to Crimea. This diminishes the

Kremlin's need to gain control of a land corridor to Crimea through Ukraine.

Known 2: Ukraine and Russia are engaged in natural gas warfare. Kiev has claimed that Russia has illegally seized four offshore Ukrainian gas fields in the Black Sea. Ukraine has also successfully sued Russia in Stockholm's arbitration court for violating natural gas supply contracts that were signed in 2009.

Known 3: Until the end of WWII, the Baltic port of Kaliningrad was the Prussian city of Konigsberg. The Kremlin prizes this Soviet imperial remnant. The exclave has a major military base and requires economic support to survive. With the goal of spurring economic growth, the Kremlin has relaxed its control of Kaliningrad's economy. However, it has not loosened the political reins. As this book is written, the Kremlin is conducting an intense information campaign against what it calls the Germanization of Kaliningrad.

Known 4: A minor dispute rages over the precise translation of Putin's April 25, 2005, statement lamenting the USSR's demise. Did he say that the Soviet collapse was "a major geo-political disaster of the [twentieth] century" or that it was the "greatest geo-political catastrophe of the century"? The BBC and NBC News chose the "catastrophe" translation. Both renditions confirm that the Soviet collapse appalled former KGB colonel Putin.

Known 5: For over a century, the Kremlin has used politically divisive and demonstrably false news reports to forward covert influence operations. *New York Times* reporter Walter Duranty won the 1932 Pulitzer Prize for his 1931 coverage of the USSR, even though his reporting was false narrative of the most hideous, immoral, and inexcusable kind. Duranty denied that Soviet dictator Josef Stalin's forced agricultural collectivization program had killed millions. In

November 1931, he denied that there was a famine or any "actual starvation" in the USSR. However, a genocidal famine was occurring. All told, violent Bolshevik repression and the famine killed from 2.5 to ten million people.

Known 6: The Soviet Union employed poisonous military, diplomatic, and information warfare cocktails. The 1983 Euromissile Crisis was a calculated Kremlin operation designed to divide NATO. As the crisis played out, the Reagan administration demonstrated that an American president can craft and execute difficult political, diplomatic, and media operations under intense pressure in order to secure strategic goals vital to American interests. To pull it off, however, the president must do three things: (1) be totally committed to achieving the strategic goals, no matter the personal and political price he may pay; (2) make absolutely certain that the organizations tasked with implementing policy are fully prepared to execute their missions; and (3) when the president commits America to international action after having secured allied support and cooperation, he must do what he says he will do.

In the 1970s, the Soviets began deploying SS-20 theater ballistic missiles in Eastern Europe. The missiles threatened western European cities and threatened NATO's critical British air bases with short-notice attack. NATO responded to Kremlin escalation with a dual-track policy pushed by the Carter administration. NATO would negotiate to remove the SS-20s but, should the Soviets refuse to withdraw them, the allies would deploy equivalent systems. West Germany's socialist chancellor, Helmut Schmidt, argued that Jimmy Carter's approach exposed NATO to Soviet political warfare designed to sap NATO's collective will to resist. Schmidt favored a common-sense response that said: "You deploy, we deploy. You negotiate, we negotiate." Carter, however, insisted on the dual track.

Carter's strategic naiveté delighted Kremlin chess masters. They saw their end game: Negotiations would fail. As Schmidt feared, neutralist sentiment, evident in Holland and Belgium, infected West Germany. Leveraging classic anti-American tropes (Adolf Hitler dismissed Americans as "cowboys"), Moscow's propagandists portrayed NATO's response to the SS-20s as the aggressive act—NATO was preparing to attack Russia. The Kremlin hoped to confuse and frighten Europeans to the point of psychological flipflop. In frightened minds, America's promise to protect Europe within its nuclear umbrella might morph into an American nuclear threat to Europe. Kremlin propagandists argued that this psychological judo could shatter NATO.

In mid-1983, having collectively concluded that negotiations had failed, NATO confirmed it would deploy US cruise missiles to Britain and Italy and Pershing 2 ballistic missiles to West Germany to counter the Soviet SS-20s.

And then the crisis, designed to stop NATO's counter-deployment, began in full media fury. Western "peace" organizations, Western pacifists, and Communist sympathizers demonstrated throughout Western Europe and the US, their protests motley, yet synchronized. In October the demonstrations intensified, along with media hysterics. Why? The West German parliament had scheduled a vote on missile deployment.

On November 22, West Germany's parliament approved the missile deployment. The next day, US missiles arrived in Europe. NATO counter-deployed—and nuclear war didn't erupt. Kremlin propagandists and chess masters…were checked.

Eighteen months later, Mikhail Gorbachev's reformist Kremlin regime accepted a deal that Reagan, the cowboy nuclear warmonger, had offered prior to the crisis—no SS-20s, no US missiles.

Two Unknowns

Unknown 1: Did Russia's decision to attack Ukraine rely on the assumption of "energy dominance" at least until 2020, if not to 2050? The Kremlin's bold actions in 2014 indicate it thought it could annex Crimea, dissect Ukraine, and maybe, just maybe, shatter NATO. Through 2013, European economies relied heavily on Russian natural gas and petroleum exports. In the middle of winter, the Kremlin could say, "Hey, you spoiled Berlin and Paris elites, kowtow or freeze." The fracking revolution—hydraulic fracturing to tap vast reservoirs of "tight" natural gas—altered the global strategic energy calculus. The US, Canada, and Mexico have enormous reserves. Europe has at least a dozen seaports capable of offloading tankers carrying liquefied natural gas. The ports have pipeline connections.

Unknown 2: Will Sweden and Finland join NATO? Kremlin belligerence has sparked a sea change in Sweden. When regional powers make political demands, smaller nations always react. Often they accommodate, perhaps appease. However, when an aggressive actor pulls its sabers—and especially when the bully actually seizes territory—good golly, sometimes small nations don't cower. Finland has also shown an inclination to cooperate militarily with NATO, but then the Finns distrust the Kremlin, so this inclination isn't a totally new phenomenon. Stay tuned. The Kremlin knows that a small nation that resists can become a huge problem. In 1940 (while still an ally of Nazi Germany), Soviet dictator Josef Stalin ordered the Red Army to attack Finland. During the Winter War, Finn ski troops cut Russian regiments to shreds.

Four Tactical, Operational, and Strategic Complexities to Ponder

Complexity 1: Serbs still regard Kosovo as the cradle of their civilization. Muslim Turks took Kosovo from Eastern Orthodox Serbs in 1389.

Complexity 2: European industries need Russian resources. This gives Russia an economic-diplomatic lever.

Complexity 3: The Crimea invasion and annexation have already established a twenty-first century political-psychological precedent: Authoritarian governments bent on territorial expansion will ignore paper documents restricting their expansion. The Budapest Memorandum of 1994 traded Ukrainian nuclear weapons for mutual security guarantees. Russia's utter disregard for the memorandum was a stunning kinetic rejection of nuclear disarmament advocates who argue that multilateral treaties provide security.

Complexity 4: NATO faces a decision-cycle situation similar to one it faced during the Cold War. When does a crisis in Eastern Europe escalate to the point that NATO must move forces east en masse? When should NATO begin bringing American forces stationed in the US to Europe?

Diplomatic and Military Scenarios

This list is meant to be illustrative. It is not complete. The scenarios are speculations, not predictions.

1. **"Permanent Frontline Freeze" in Eastern Ukraine:** This complex scenario has numerous variables, but long-term Russian economic stagnation is a key one. Oil's price plunge has already limited Russian options; if oil prices remain relatively low, Ukraine's frozen war may continue. Retreating from Ukraine would deeply embarrass Russian oligarchs. A permanent quagmire in eastern Ukraine is more acceptable, as long as mercenaries and separatists take the casualties. (Russia has accepted a frozen-war situation in Moldova's Transdniestr.)

2. **Peace Enforcement Operation in Ukraine:** A peacekeeping intervention has advocates in the UN, Europe, and Asia. The proposed operation has numerous problems. Which nations will be allowed to provide peacekeeping troops? Russian and NATO peacekeepers are presumably non-starters. Ireland, Finland, Austria, and Switzerland might be acceptable European contributors. After that, it gets thin. Algeria? Perhaps not, too prone to French influence. Angola? Maybe. Argentina has advocates. Vietnam? Possibly—if China doesn't veto Vietnamese participation. Another pertinent question at the operational and tactical levels of military existence: Could these nations provide the estimated 2030,000 troops the operation would require and the equipment they would need to deter a mechanized attack by Russia? Assuming the force could be assembled and properly equipped, how and where would it deploy? The rules of engagement (ROE) for peacekeepers would be an endless debate in the UN. (A ROE describes the circumstances in which soldiers can use deadly force.)

3. **The Baltic Thrust:** This is a Russian offensive scenario. Russian forces would most likely attack west from Belarus toward Kaliningrad. Lithuania and a sliver of Polish territory known

as the Suwalki Gap separate Belarus from Kaliningrad, so triggering NATO Article 5 is a possibility. The Baltic Thrust might target Estonia from Russian territory. The attack on Estonia would combine a Crimea-type unconventional attack with a conventional assault featuring tanks and mechanized infantry supported by air strikes.

4. **The War for the RUBK:** A pragmatic, sane, non-megalomaniacal Kremlin version of this scenario starts with a strategic distraction operation. To distract American and world media attention, the Kremlin foments a dangerous crisis in another area. Perhaps the crisis flares in the South China Sea, or Korea, or the Middle East, or North Africa. Perhaps Turkish and Greek forces clash in the Aegean, or Iranian proxies in southern Lebanon attack Israel with chemical weapons. A stretch but not totally implausible—the Kremlin bribes corrupt Iranian Revolutionary Guard Corps units to launch a limited ballistic missile attack (conventional warheads only) on Saudi Arabian oilfields. The Kremlin has other malign and destructive options. The distraction operation could force an American military deployment to the crisis region and perhaps the deployment of other NATO forces as well (particularly French, British, and German).

Meanwhile, back in the ex-USSR: While Russian Army forces engage in military exercises with Belarusian forces, the Kremlin launches a pro-Russian coup in Belarus. The coup quickly succeeds and Minsk remains calm. In Ukraine, however, the Kremlin stages a bloody "false flag" incident in which dozens of Russian nationals are killed. After twenty-four hours of agitation propaganda accusing Ukraine of mass murdering ethnic Russians and committing other genocidal crimes,

Russia launches a tank-led attack on western Ukraine, with Kiev as the primary objective. It simultaneously launches the Baltic Thrust offensive from Belarus to Kaliningrad.

The likely outcome: a major war in Eastern Europe.

5. **Cold War Revival:** In some respects, this is already occurring. However, Russia has a weak hand in Cold War II. The Kremlin oligarchs have no ideological lever. Russian nationalism and imperial revival lack the pseudo-intellectual cachet of international Communism. If NATO acts in concert, even with nuclear weapons Russia is at a severe disadvantage.

CHAPTER 5

PROXY AND TRIBAL COMBAT AMID ENDEMIC DESPERATION

Iran Exploits Yemen's Nest of Wars

Yemen's complex nest of wars is a hideous but representative example of a bloody, chaotic tragedy exploited by an expanding power, in this case the Iranian Shia Islamic revolutionary dictatorship established in 1979 by the Grand Ayatollah Ruhollah Khomeini.

Iran and Al Qaeda use chaotic Yemen as a base for operations throughout the Arabian peninsula and along Africa's Red Sea littoral. Yemeni instability also provides a type of plausible deniability. Iran can blame its own bombings, assassinations, attacks on shipping, and even missile launches on indigenous Yemeni insurgents.

Yemen's geographical proximity attracts the Iranian clerical dictatorship. Yemen is the back door to petro-power Saudi Arabia, a regional and ethnic rival that the Iranian clerics despise. Pitiful Yemen? Wealthy Saudi Arabia? Both are stepping stones to reviving

Iranian (neo-Persian) Great Power status. This off-beat chapter assessing an illustrative but off-the-radar war includes a grim timeline detailing Yemen's tragic chaos and Iran's violent meddling.

Chapter Abbreviation Key

ABM = Anti-ballistic missile

AQAP = Al Qaeda in the Arabian Peninsula

GCC = Gulf Cooperation Council

IRGC = Islamic Revolutionary Guard Corps

JCPOA = Joint Comprehensive Plan of Action (the July 2015 Iran nuclear weapons agreement negotiated by the Obama administration between the UN Security Council's five permanent members and Germany, the P5+1)

OPEC = Organization of Petroleum Exporting Countries

PAC-3 = Patriot advanced capability 3. U.S.-made short-range anti-missile missile

UAV = Unmanned aerial vehicle (drone)

Overview of Iran's Deadly Meddling: Agitation, Terror, Crime, and Proxy Wars in the Gray Zone

Iran's clerical dictatorship knows it confronts serious internal challenges. Though loath to admit it, the dictatorship recognizes its conventional military inferiority compared to its many adversaries, particularly Israel, the US, and Turkey. The Sunni Arab Gulf Cooperation Council (GCC) states are acquiring modern weapons and improving the skills of their conventional forces. Hyperpower America supports Israel and the GCC states. Though diplomatic relations between Ankara and Washington have deteriorated since 2011—and the Syrian war has played a role in that—Turkey and the US are NATO allies.

Until nuclear weapons and ICBMs compensate for its conventional weaknesses, in its pursuit of grandiose strategic goals the Iranian regime employs a variety of cocktail operations to disrupt, antagonize, potentially weaken, and perhaps fatally wound its stronger adversaries. The ayatollahs hope these operations keep regional adversaries off balance and frustrate Great Powers (like the US) seeking regional stability. Violent meddling operations demonstrate the regime's ruthlessness; the dictatorship thinks these vicious operations have deterrent value, domestically and internationally.

To avoid provoking a regime-threatening conventional war with a stronger adversary or stronger coalition, the dictatorship's meddling operations usually rely on covert operatives and proxy forces with no overt direct link to Tehran. Proxies provide plausible deniability, which propaganda and diplomacy can reinforce.

Tehran's Gray Zone Cocktails: A Primer

Iranian "gray-zone cocktails" combine political influence and agitation campaigns, criminal activities that undermine local authority (especially bribery, smuggling, and drug trafficking), and cyber warfare. Iranian operatives provide financial resources, technical assistance, material aid (including weapons), and intelligence information to militants of all ideological and ethnic stripes. Iranian personnel and proxy agents conduct covert and occasionally overt military operations using unconventional and conventional warfare capabilities; they may conduct terror attacks and assassinations. Larger hybrid operations—when the stakes are worth the risk— employ proxy forces, Iranian special forces, and modern weapons, to include short and intermediate-range ballistic missiles. Local sympathizers provide these operations with intelligence, clandestine cover, and plausible deniability.

Iran has employed these techniques throughout the world, from Iraq to the Balkans to South America to Southeast Asia to Afghanistan—a world tour.

Four conflicts in which Iran—for better or worse—is deeply involved are proxy wars in which associated violence and destruction defy plausible deniability: Iran's war in neighboring Iraq, the war in wretched Syria, Lebanon's unsettled conflict, and chaotic Yemen's nest of wars.

Key Actors, Their Goals and Risks

Iran

Regime Decision-Making: The Islamic republic's supreme leader has ultimate authority in Iran. He decides. The supreme leader must be a senior Shia Muslim cleric. Once chosen by the Assembly of Experts, he is not term-limited (though the Assembly of Experts could remove him). Two appointed councils control policy formulation, major legislation, and elections: the Council of Guardians and the Expediency Council. Regime-approved Shia clerics dominate both panels. The clerisy also controls wealthy religious foundations called bonyads, which own valuable businesses and real estate in Iran. Bonyads are largely exempt from taxation.

Most Important Regime Strategic Goal: Regime maintenance. The regime relies on two organizations for protection. They also play key roles in regime gray-zone operations.

Islamic Revolutionary Guard Corps: Created by the Ayatollah Khomeini after the 1979 revolution to protect his regime against a coup by pro-Shah, liberal, democratic, and leftist officers in the Iranian military. Today IRGC's one hundred and fifty-thousand guardsmen defend Khomeini's Islamic republic against internal and external threats. It operates air and naval units and controls the Basij Resistance Force, a paramilitary organization with one million fighters. It provides personnel for regime gray-zone operations. Its personnel train proxy fighters. The IRGC works closely with the Ministry of Intelligence and Security (MOIS), which conducts domestic surveillance operations against regime opponents. Corruption has sullied IRGC revolutionary purity. IRGC officers have used their power to gain economic clout. They can influence strategic industries (including the oil industry), communications services, and legitimate businesses (including real estate transactions). They definitely participate in black-market operations.

Al Quds Force: Elite arm of the IRGC. Controls Iran's international covert and irregular warfare operations and oversees its ballistic missile units. Has ten thousand to fifteen thousand people.

Strategic Goal and Strategic Narrative: Khomeini's Islamic republic seeks Great Power status and ultimately global domination.

Strategic Goal: Acquire nuclear weapons and delivery systems. Great Powers China and Russia have nuclear weapons. Would-be Great Power Iran covets them. Nuclear weapons will threaten Arab states, Europe, the US, and, of course, Israel. The Israelis, however, have made it clear that they will use everything they have, including nuclear weapons, to defend themselves from an Iranian attack.

Strategic Goal in Yemen: Vex and weaken Saudi Arabia by attacking the kingdom from its Yemeni back door. Iran does not need to completely control Yemen to do this. Yemen is another location from which to launch attacks on Israel and Egypt.

Iranian Oil Choke-Point Military and Economic Operations: Iran is already able to close the Strait of Hormuz, which connects the Persian Gulf and the Indian Ocean. Yemen is on the eastern side of the Bab el-Mandeb (Gateway of Anguish), the twenty-two mile wide strait connecting the Red Sea and the Indian Ocean. Every day tankers bearing millions of barrels of oil pass through the strait. Close it using naval mines, anti-ship missiles, "swarm boat" attacks, and perhaps submarines, and the price of oil will spike. Threatening to interfere also can spike prices. (See the following Military Scenario 2.) Yemeni rebels have launched sporadic attack on tankers in the Red Sea.

Diplomatic and Military Goals in Iraq and Syria: Prevent Sunnis from regaining power and dominate the Iraqi and Syrian regimes controlling their respective countries. Iran has already made Lebanese Hezbollah the dominant political and military force in Lebanon. If possible, use pro-Iranian forces in Syria to attack Israel.

Follow-Up Strategic Diplomatic and Military Goals: Create the "Shia crescent," an Iranian-dominated land route extending to the Mediterranean Sea. This crescent would run from Iran through Iraq, Syria, and Lebanon. This would facilitate more proxy attacks on Israel. Lebanon is a political mess. However, recent seismic studies indicate it could have substantial offshore natural gas reserves. One of its potential areas is in an area that Israel also claims to control. Iran could easily exploit this dispute with information warfare operations portraying Iran as a defender of Muslim interests.

Saudi Arabia

Strategic Goal: Prevent Iranian (neo-Persian) domination in Yemen, in the Gulf, in Iraq, and in Africa.

Strategic Internal Political, Economic, and Cultural Goal: The Kingdom is pursuing systemic social and economic modernization. New Saudi leaders have concluded dependence on oil income is a long-term vulnerability.

Strategic Goal of Saud Tribe: Retain control of Saudi Arabia and its territory.

Military, Diplomatic, Economic, and Information Operational Goals: Continue to dominate GCC. Find ways to cooperate militarily, economically, and diplomatically with Israel without inciting Sunni conservatives.

Yemen Government

Strategic Goal: Reach an internal political accommodation that ends the violent conflicts.

Yemen Rebels

There are many rebel groups and they have different goals: The timeline sub-section introduces the major rebel groups and discusses illustrative rebel military and political goals.

Israel

Strategic Goals: Deny the Iranian dictatorship nuclear weapons. End the Iranian regime's ability to conduct attacks on Israel using proxy actors (such as rocket attacks by the Lebanese group Hezbollah on Israel).

Arab Persian Gulf States

They are not a block. Bahrain, Oman, and Qatar play a game of diplomatically balancing between Iran and Saudi Arabia.

United States

Official Objectives in Yemen: Restore the UN-recognized Yemen government and protect Saudi territorial integrity from rebel incursion.

Intelligence Operations: The US has provided intelligence, military advice, and logistical support to the Saudi-led coalition.

The Embargo: The US participates in the naval blockade, a military-economic-diplomatic operation. American naval vessels have had to deal with naval mines and explosive unmanned boat attacks.

Economic and Diplomatic Operations: Washington has imposed harsh sanctions on the Islamic Revolutionary Guard Corps (IRGC), citing its continued support to the Syrian regime of Bashar al-Assad and the aid it continues to provide to Hezbollah.

America's Military Advantage: The US Central Command (CENTCOM) controls US forces in Syria, Iraq, Afghanistan, Yemen, and the Persian Gulf region. The US 5th Fleet (CENTCOM's naval component) has its headquarters in Bahrain. US military forces are by far the most powerful in the region.

Great Britain

From 1839 to 1967, the southern city-state of Aden was a British colony. Aden was a member of the Federation of South Arabia, a loosely organized concoction Britain created in 1959. Many southern Yemeni sultanates and governorates refused to join the federation. Two militant organizations led the political fight for southern independence, the Marxist National Liberation Front and the Arab nationalist Front for the Liberation of Occupied South Yemen. When Britain withdrew, the southerners formed the People's

Democratic Republic of Yemen (PDRY), a state separate from the northern Yemen Arab Republic.

The British still have relationships with several southern tribes, including members of pro-secession factions. The relationships have diplomatic and intelligence benefits. Britain has provided intelligence, training, and other covert support to the Saudi-led coalition.

Turkey

A traditional Iranian adversary. Turkish objectives in Iraq and Syria clash with Iranian goals. From the late sixteenth century to 1918, Yemen troubled the Ottoman Empire. In 1849, the Ottomans returned to northern Yemen in force after the British occupied Aden.

NATO

NATO is a coalition partner in Iraq and Syria. It seeks to deny Iran bases on the Mediterranean and Red Seas.

Russia

Russia is very engaged in Syria and operates as a quasi-Iranian ally, since Moscow and Tehran support the Assad regime.

Economic Goal: The Russian and Iranian economies rely on oil export income. Both nations benefit from price spikes.

Military and Diplomatic Cooperation with Iran: Russia provides Iran with advanced air defense weapons that would complicate a US strike on Iranian nuclear facilities. In 2015, Iran and Russia signed "an agreement to expand military cooperation." The deal includes counter-terror cooperation, military training, and "enabling each country's navy to use the other's ports more frequently."

Information-Military Cocktail: The Kremlin has suggested that Russian warships would defend Iranian ports against all aggressors. Russia is implying it support Iran in a Strait of Hormuz closure scenario.

Diplomatic Risks: In Syria, Russia considers Iran to be an ally—a flawed ally, but a useful one. However, Russia does not want Iran to start a major war with Israel, Syria, or any other country. Russian diplomats have criticized Tehran for demanding Israel's destruction. They add, however, that when it comes to challenging Israel, the Iranian regime completely disregards Russian, Turkish, and American warnings to cease and desist.

China

Iran thinks China's Belt and Road Initiative is an attractive proposition. China has provided diplomatic support for Iran in the UN, including weakening economic and political sanction requests by the US, Saudi Arabia, and Great Britain.

Wild Cards

North Korea: Pyongyang has aided Iran's nuclear and ballistic missile programs.

Yemen's Hell Cocktail: Yemen is a nest of wars within wars, a violent, wicked geo-political problem so volatile, fluid, and variable that some commentators refer to it as a "chaos state."

Yemen has very powerful internal enemies—enemies such as poverty, hunger, overpopulation, water shortages, corruption, unemployment, drug addiction, and a primitive, unproductive economy. The list continues.

Other regional wars complicate Yemen's hunger problem. Over a million African refugees have fled to Yemen, about half of them from war-ravaged Somalia. Caring for them would burden Yemen in peace, much less in the midst of chaotic warfare.

Over the past twenty years the Iranian dictatorship has exploited and exacerbated Yemen's preexisting wars and vulnerabilities. Yemen is an attractive strategic location for Iranian troublemaking. It is a second front in Iran's war with Saudi Arabia. The Bab el-Mandeb strait is another oil-tanker choke point.

Timeline Capturing Critical and Illustrative Events

This historical timeline provides important background information and illustrative examples of participants' actions and operations. The details support the Yemen's Wars Within Wars section.

Note: Yemen's northern rebels are known by two names: Ansar Allah (Partisans of God) and the Houthis. They belong to the Zaidi sect of Shia Islam (Zaidism). The Houthis advocate an eclectic political agenda. They demand political autonomy in northern Yemen. They oppose corruption. As a sectarian organization, they try to avoid identification with a particular tribe. They oppose foreign intervention—but receive Iranian support.

June–September 2004: **Major Event:** In northern Yemen, government security forces battle Ansar Allah insurgents led by Shia cleric Hussein Badreddin al-Houthi. He is killed in September. The insurgents begin to use their deceased leader's family name as a name for their movement.

March 2005–December 2006: Fighting erupts between the government and Hussein al-Houthi loyalists. His brother, Abdul Malik al-Houthi, now leads the movement. In May, the rebels agree to end the rebellion. However, low-level violence persists. Houthi fighters claim that government officials in the north are corrupt. In March 2006, the government frees over six hundred Shia who fought for Hussein al-Houthi. They receive amnesty.

January 2007–mid-2009: Intermittent fighting flares between government forces and Houthis. Ceasefire agreements are made and then broken.

January 2009: Al Qaeda in Saudi Arabia and Yemen unite to form Al Qaeda in the Arabian Peninsula. AQAP's major bases are in Yemen. Like the Iranian regime, AQAP opposes the House of Saud which rules Saudi Arabia.

August 2009: The government begins a major offensive against Shia rebels in Saada province (northern Yemen, the Houthis' home province). AQAP tries to murder Saudi prince Mohammed bin Nayef.

October–November 2009: **Major Event:** Saudi Arabian police kill two AQAP terrorists attempting to enter Saudi Arabia from Yemen. In early November, Yemeni rebels cross the border and kill a Saudi policeman. Saudi combat aircraft bomb a rebel base in Yemen. The Saudis accuse the rebels of aiding Al Qaeda. The rebels tell Saudi Arabia to stay out of Yemen. These events have major consequences.

September 2010: As a ceasefire holds in the north, government forces launch an offensive against Sunni separatists in Shabwah province. Shabwah is in the southern Hadhramaut region. Osama bin Laden's family came from the Hadhramaut.

December 2010: The northern ceasefire crumbles as Houthi rebels battle government troops.

January–August 2011: Demonstrations flare in Yemen, sparked by Tunisia's Arab Spring rebellion. Intermittent clashes continue to occur between government security forces and Houthi rebels in the north. In June a rocket fired on Sanaa wounds President Ali Abdullah Saleh. Saleh is a Zaidi Shia. However, Houthi rebels condemn him for dealing with Yemen's Sunni majority. In August, protestors from throughout Yemen demonstrate in Sanaa and demand more regional autonomy. Houthi demonstrators demand political autonomy in the north.

September 2011–February 2012: Several disgruntled senior military officers defect to the rebels. Though military units and police forces remain loyal to the central government, many of their commanders argue that a new national unity government will calm the country. President Saleh has been in power for thirty-two years.

Major Event: In November 2011, Saleh agrees to resign. Vice president Abd-Rabbu Mansour Hadi will head a national unity government that includes the political opposition. In February 2012, Hadi is elected president. However, fighting between the government and Shia rebels continues. The government also attacks Sunni separatists in the south.

October 2012–March 2013: Hadi's government accuses Iran of supporting Shia rebels in the north and Sunni separatists in the south. In March 2013, a naval vessel enforcing the embargo off Yemen's northern Red Sea coast catches a freighter transferring weapons to a smaller fishing boat. Investigators later conclude that the weapons came from Iran.

April 2013: Tribesmen in Marib province attack electrical transmission lines and cause a blackout in Sanaa. They also attack the two-hundred-mile-long oil pipeline running from Marib's oil fields to Hodeida. The government estimates that since spring 2011, attacks on the pipeline have cost Yemen four billion dollars in lost revenue.

May 2013: Armed secessionists clash with government forces near the southern seaport of Aden. In the southern port of Taiz, police seize a ship carrying twenty thousand illegal weapons and ammunition. Authorities believe the shipment came through Turkey.

June 2013: The government accuses the Houthi rebels of sending several hundred men to Syria to defend the Assad government. The Shia fighters travel to Lebanon. The Lebanese group Hezbollah equips and organizes the Houthi fighters for combat in Syria. The government has evidence that Iran pays the Houthis fighting in Syria.

September 2013: Oil pipeline attacks continue. Each attack requires from one to seven days to repair. The Marib pipeline carries 125,000 barrels a day to the export terminal. Oil royalty revenue losses mount quickly.

November 2013: In the north, Shia tribesmen attack pro-government Sunni fighters manning roadblocks. The roadblocks hinder food and fuel shipments to the Shia tribes. The war of the roadblocks began in late October 2013. By late November, over two hundred have been killed and some six hundred wounded in roadblock combat. During the month, China offers to increase investment in Yemen and build infrastructure if the government demonstrates it can protect Chinese workers in Yemen.

February 2014: A government commission approves a recommendation to restructure Yemen. It will become a federation with six semi-autonomous regions. Houthi rebels reject it.

April 2014: In the southern port city of Mukalla, several thousand demonstrators demand re-establishing the separate state of Southern Yemen. During the month, US drone attacks kill some twenty-five AQAP terrorists based in south Yemen.

July 2014: Due to the loss of oil-export income, Hadi's government decides it does not have the money to continue to subsidize fuel prices. Oil and electricity subsidies consume thirty percent of government income. Foreign-aid donors had been pressuring the government to cut them. The price of gas immediately rises sixty percent. Houthi rebels launch attacks in northern and central Yemen. Rebels take Amran, north of Sanaa, as its army garrison flees. Rebel forces move within twenty-two miles of Sanaa. Rebels attempt to seize a hill overlooking Sanaa's international airport, but Sunni fighters loyal to the government stop them.

August–September 2014: The fuel-price rise sparks anti-government demonstrations in Sanaa. Thousands of Shia Houthis participate in the demonstrations. **Major Event:** Houthi rebels enter the capital. The government orders them to disarm, but they refuse. Fighting breaks out in the capital. Government forces refuse to fight an urban battle that would kill civilians and cause massive damage. Facing little armed resistance, Houthi rebels seize several neighborhoods; they kill at least three hundred people. By mid-September, the Shia rebels control most of the city. Houthi leaders say they will not withdraw until Hadi forms a new government with a new, independent prime minister. On September 21, the Houthis and the government agree to a peace deal that includes a revealing demand: The government must free several jailed Iranians and Shia Arabs whom it had jailed and charged with being agents of the Iranian government. On September 24, the government frees two Lebanese nationals accused of being members of Hezbollah. On September 25, it releases three Iranians accused of being Iranian secret police and eight Yemeni Shia charged with smuggling Iranian weapons into Yemen. The peace deal halts the street battles.

October 2014: Houthi fighters fully control Sanaa. They demand that Hadi resign. Iran praises what it calls a Shia victory. By the end of the month, Shia rebels also control Sanaa and all or part of nine of Yemen's twenty-two provinces. Yemen's army and its hapless government still exist. However, military opposition to Houthi rebels is weak, and the Houthis have trapped the government in Sanaa. In mid-month, Shia rebels capture Harad, a major town on the Saudi border. The GCC declares that Yemen cannot be allowed to disintegrate. At the end of the month, the US provides an explanation for Yemeni military inaction. Washington believes that former dictator Saleh and his allies in the security forces are cooperating with the Houthis.

November 2014: Rebels seize the seaport of Hodeida (Hudaydah). Rebel forces also advance south. To appease the rebels and keep Yemen from disintegrating, the UN attempts to assemble a dream-team unity government in Sanaa.

2015—the Critical Year

January 2015: Thirty thousand Sunni tribesmen in Marib province prepare to fight the Shia rebels. **Major Event:** On January 20, Houthis in Sanaa seize the presidential palace. The presidential guard does not resist. The Houthis briefly take Hadi prisoner. Hadi agrees to give the Houthis more autonomy in the north. On January 22, he resigns. In late January, an American drone attack kills Harith an-Nadhari, a senior AQAP leader.

February 2015: The Houthis reject a proposed new constitution. They dissolve the parliament and announce that a Presidential Council will replace Hadi. A National Council will replace the parliament. Three Russian-made ground-attack aircraft purchased from Belarus arrive in Hodeida—they are for the Houthi rebels. On February 21, Hadi flees to Aden.

March 2015: For the first time since 1990, a direct flight from Iran lands in Yemen. Iran claims the plane carries humanitarian aid. The World Bank shutters its Yemen operations, denying the Houthi government access to World Bank loans. Sunni tribes, secular political parties, and southern secessionists form an anti-Shia coalition, the National Salvation Bloc. On March 19, an Iranian freighter unloads 185 tons of weapons and equipment in the port of Saleef. Houthi forces advancing south to Aden take the port of Taiz. Hadi, from Aden, asks the GCC for help. He asks the UN to declare a no-fly zone over Yemen. Russia and China stall UN action.

March 25, 2018: Shia rebels enter Aden and clash with pro-government tribesmen. Hadi flees to Saudi Arabia.

March 26, 2015: **Major Event:** a Saudi Arabian-led coalition of Arab states intervenes on behalf of Hadi's government. Over a hundred warplanes from Saudi Arabia, the UAE, and Bahrain target the Houthi advance on Aden and Houthi supply centers. The coalition also includes Egypt, Jordan, Sudan, Morocco, Kuwait, and Qatar. Egyptian public opinion indicates that Egyptians support providing aircraft and warships but not ground troops. The coalition imposes a naval blockade. The blockade closes the port of Hodeida. Iran had agreed to help the Shia rebels modernize and upgrade Hodeida. However, the coalition embargo puts the agreement on hold.

April 2015: Pro-government tribesmen defending Aden capture two Iranian military advisers. An Iranian convoy with two small warships and seven small freighters bearing supplies for Yemen encounters a US Navy task force off Oman. The convoy returns to

Iran. Saudi Arabia hastily declares that its coalition controls all sea, land, and air access to Yemen. The Saudis also claim that the coalition has destroyed the majority of known rebel military facilities. Facts on the ground don't support the claims. As April ends, Saudi Arabia has over two hundred thousand soldiers on its border with Yemen.

May 2015: Heavy fighting continues around Aden. Pro-government forces hold the port facility. Senegal joins the Saudi coalition. On May 9, the Saudi coalition conducts over a hundred air strikes. Observers estimate that the air offensive has caused over ten thousand casualties since it began. One-third are civilian. Six hundred thousand people have fled western Yemen to avoid air attacks. In Sanaa, the air strikes have destroyed over two thousand structures. The coalition claims they are military facilities (warehouses). From May 13 to 17, the UN arranges a brief "humanitarian pause." UN ships pass through the naval blockade. Despite a few firefights, during the ceasefire truck convoys deliver supplies from rebel-controlled Hodeida and government-controlled Aden. When the ceasefire ends, air strikes and ground combat resume.

June 2015: On June 4, a major diplomatic event occurs: Saudi Arabia publicly acknowledges that it has met secretly with Israel. The Saudis explain that both nations have mutual concerns about Iran. Later in June, Houthis fire a Scud ballistic missile at a Saudi air base. Patriot ABMs intercept the Scud. An American missile fired by a UAV kills AQAP commander Nasser al-Wuhayshi.

July 2015: Civilian casualties from air strikes continue to mount. The US receives criticism since it is no secret that America is providing the Saudi coalition air campaign with intelligence and supplies. Relief agencies estimate that ten to eleven million Yemenis (slightly less than half the total population) need food assistance. In mid-month, government forces take full control of Aden and rebels begin to withdraw to the north. The Saudis report that since April, fighting along the Saudi-Yemen border has killed two hundred people. At the end of July, a hacker group calling itself the YCA (Yemen Cyber Army) attacks Saudi government email systems.

August 2015: The Saudi-led coalition acknowledges that a mechanized combat brigade of three thousand soldiers and over a hundred armored vehicles arrived by sea in Aden on August 2 and quickly offloaded. On August 4, the so-called Arab Brigade seized Al Anad air base in Lahij province. About half of the brigade's personnel come from the UAE. Saudi Arabian tanks serve with the brigade. At least two Saudi mechanized battalion task forces have entered northern Yemen. Another mechanized battalion has entered southeastern Yemen. At bases near Aden, Saudi, Emirati, Egyptian, and Jordanian military advisers are training government forces.

September 2015: **Major Event:** On September 4, a rebel missile launched from a site near Sanaa hits an ammo facility on a government air base in Marib province. The explosion kills forty-five UAE soldiers and ten Saudis in the Arab Brigade. Another 150 are wounded. Government forces, led by a vengeful Arab Brigade, drive north toward Sanaa. Coalition air strikes increase and fighting becomes more intense. President Hadi returns to Aden.

October 2015: As Shia rebels retreat toward Sanaa, Iran accuses the Saudi coalition of war crimes. Sunni Arab soldiers regain control of the Bab el-Mandab strait, in the Gulf of Aden, between Yemen and Djibouti. Despite Iranian objections, Sudan deploys ground troops in Yemen. Sudan and Iran were once allies, but Sudan is a Sunni Muslim state. Hadi leaves Aden after terrorists attack the hotel in which he lives.

November 2015: Trouble breaks out among pro-government Sunni tribes, frustrating Saudi coalition operations. Hadi returns to Aden again. In late November, four hundred foreign mercenaries serving in the UAE deploy to Yemen. The UAE has a mercenary battalion of eight hundred "contract" western military veterans it uses as a counter-terror unit.

December 2015: In early December, government forces seize commercial trucks carrying several tons of Iranian weapons and ammo. Fishing boats evade the blockade and deliver the military supplies to a small port on the southern Yemen coast. Former president Saleh admits he supports the Shia rebels. Several hundred Shia rebels raid the Saudi Arabian province of Jizan. Saudi security forces respond and kill over two hundred people. However, the raiders remain in the province two weeks before withdrawing. UN efforts to establish a ceasefire fail. Saudi Patriot ABMs intercept another ballistic missile fired from Yemen.

January 2016: Britain admits that British personnel in Yemen are providing intelligence assistance to pro-government forces.

February 2016–mid-2016: Chaotic warfare continues. In April 2016, the UN sponsors new negotiations between the Hadi government and the Houthis. The Houthi coalition now includes former president Saleh's General People's Congress (GPC). Captured rebel commanders admit that Hezbollah and Iranian personnel run military training camps in the north (Saada province). The coalition deploys Patriot ABMs around government bases in Marib province.

November–December 2016: The Saudi coalition and Yemeni government forces slowly drive rebels' positions along the Red Sea coast. Heavy fighting occurs around Taiz. Rebels continue to hold Hodeida.

January 2017: UN and other international agencies estimate that fighting since March 2015 has killed twelve thousand people and wounded over thirty thousand. Three million people have fled their homes and remain displaced (they are internally displaced people, or IDPs). The staggering statistic: Sixteen to seventeen million people (out of a population of twenty-five million) now depend on international food aid to survive. Much of that aid flows through Hodeida.

February–March 2017: A Saudi Patriot missile intercepts a ballistic missile fired by Shia rebels aimed at a base near Riyadh. The coalition declares Hodeida a war zone and says foreign organizations operating in the port should act accordingly. Rebels attempt to retake the smaller ports of Midi (north of Hodeida) and Mocha. They fail. However, the rebels continue to hold Hodeida. Aid organizations estimate at least seventy percent of relief supplies for Yemen enter through the port.

December 2017: **Major Event:** Former president Ali Abdullah Saleh is slain during a firefight in Sanaa. American warships in the Red Sea intercept an unmanned Shark 33 patrol boat carrying explosives. Rebels directed the "robot boat" toward blockading warships.

January 2018: Seven million Yemenis are completely cut off from international food aid. Saudi Arabia transfers two billion dollars to Yemen's central bank to support the exchange rate of Yemeni currency and keep prices from rising. The coalition maritime blockade force intercepts another unmanned Shark 33 patrol boat heading toward coalition warships off the coast. The bomb boat has an Iranian guidance system. Southern separatists attack government facilities in Aden. Coalition air strikes destroy hidden rebel ammunition storage sites in Sanaa. During the month of January, the US launches air attacks on nine Al Qaeda in the Arabian Peninsula targets and one attack on an Islamic State base.

February 2018: Saudi Arabia concludes that operations in Yemen demonstrate that the Saudi Air Force, Navy, and Air Defense forces are competent. The ground forces are not.

March 2018: Saudi and Shia rebel officials admit that since January they have held secret peace negotiations in Oman. This angers the Yemeni government. However, the rebels refuse to agree to a unity government. The Houthis demand autonomy for the north, and they want to control Sanaa. The Saudi move in January to support Yemen's central bank appears to have worked. The Yemeni rial increases in value.

June 2018 Update: As the month begins, the Houthis hold Sanaa and coalition forces continue an advance on Hodeida that started in mid-May. The Hodeida offensive is an operational cocktail. Hodeida is definitely a military (M) objective; the city is the headquarters for Houthi operations on the Red Sea coast and the key Iran-Houthi logistical node. It also has immense humanitarian (H) value. The seaport is the primary transshipment point for humanitarian aid; ships offload at Hodeida and truck convoys approved by international inspectors deliver the food and medicine to the hinterland. Like the port of Aden, it is a source of tariff revenue (E for economic). Taking Hodeida has information power (I). As coalition forces reach the outskirts, the pro-coalition government announces negotiations have failed. UN officials request a ceasefire to protect civilians and port facilities and later suggest the UN assume control of port operations. The coalition says it will try to minimize damage to civilian areas. Mid-month the coalition takes Hodeida's airport; however, sporadic Houthi counterattacks continue in the area. As coalition forces probe the city center, Houthis occupy fortified positions within city neighborhoods, indicating they seek high-casualty house-to-house combat. Can it be avoided? As the month proceeds, the coalition effectively isolates the port area. Though Houthis still slip through the cordon, limiting ingress and egress gives the coalition de facto control of major shipments through the seaport. This complicates Iran's already intricate (and risky) smuggling operations along Yemen's northern Red Sea coast; supplying its proxies is more difficult. Hodeida is also a huge diplomatic (D) bargaining chip for pro-coalition Yemenis in negotiations to determine future Yemeni political arrangements. Meanwhile, Iranian Yemeni proxies fire missiles at Saudi Arabian cities; two are intercepted by ABMs near Riyadh. The coalition claims it killed eight Lebanese Hezbollah militiamen in a battle in the Saada region (Houthi territory, northwest Yemen). The Saudi–Iran war continues.

Yemen's Wars Within Wars

Yemen's multiple wars, like the multiple wars fought in Syria, have produced a major humanitarian disaster. From 2011 to 2018, an estimated four-hundred and fifty thousand were killed in Syria's wars. In comparison, twelve thousand to fifteen thousand have been killed in Yemen since March 2015. How many have been killed since the Shia Houthi insurgents fought the government in 2004? No one knows. Yemen's comparative isolation and internal disorganization frustrate the collection of accurate data. Yet in many respects, Yemen's tragedy is more reflective of warfare in less-developed countries, such as South Sudan and Congo. Food is a major weapon in Yemen.

As I write this book, starvation threatens some seventeen million of Yemen's twenty-five million people.

The War for Southern Secession: Southern Yemen once existed as a separate country. For twenty-three years, Yemen's eight southern governorates were the PDRY. In 1990, the PDRY merged with the northern Yemen Arab Republic. Check the timeline: Southern Sunni tribes routinely fight the central government for autonomy. Many southerners favor full secession. So do members of the STC (South Transitional Council). Since 2015, southern secessionist groups have become more organized and much more heavily armed. The Saudis oppose dividing Yemen. The UAE may not.

The Houthi Shia Northern Tribal Autonomy War: The timeline covers this rebellion in some detail. There are about nine million Shia in Yemen (forty percent of the population), and, like the rebels, most belong to the Zaidi sect.

The Saleh Loyalist Insurgency: Former president/dictator Ali Abdullah Saleh lost power in 2012, then decided he wanted it back. He was killed in December 2017. However, he still has supporters among Shia militias and in government security forces.

War on Sunni Militant Islamist Terror Organizations: Al Qaeda in the Arabian Peninsula (AQAP) has its headquarters in Yemen. The timeline above concentrates on Yemen's civil war. Since 2001, the US and its anti-terror coalition have conducted operations in Yemen. Unmanned aerial vehicle (UAV, or drone) attacks on Al Qaeda and Islamic State terrorists are the most common kinetic military operation in this war. In September 2011, a raid on an Al Qaeda camp in southeastern Yemen killed cleric, Al Qaeda recruiter, and American traitor Anwar al-Awlaki. In 2018, the US Department of Defense revealed that during 2017 the US launched 131 airstrikes in Yemen, 125 against Al Qaeda in the Arabian Peninsula, and six against Islamic State targets.

The Iran–Saudi Proxy War

This is the most dangerous conflict in Yemen, but Yemen is only one of this war's many theaters. The kinetic battlefield extends from Africa to Iran; the financial battlefield is global. The Yemen proxy war involves modern strike aircraft, smart weapons, ballistic missiles, and anti-missile missiles. It features a major naval blockade of Yemen's Red Sea and Indian Ocean coastlines. The kinetic proxy war in Yemen could escalate and spread to the belligerents' Persian Gulf "front yard," with Iran and the GCC Arab states confronting one another directly. The Yemen proxy war is a war within the Sunni-Shia intra-Muslim war. Iranian and Saudi narrative warfare operations target the planet's one billion Muslims. Iran is the most populous Shia nation. Wahhabi Sunni Saudi Arabia guards Islam's holiest sites, Mecca and Medina. The Iranian regime thinks it should control these holy sites.

Peace Negotiation, Ceasefire, and Humanitarian-Aid Political Warfare

This is economic, diplomatic, and information warfare shaped and shattered by the kinetic military action. The UN is a major actor in this conflict. On at least three occasions (late 2016, early 2017, and early 2018), UN officials indicated that Shia rebels were interested in a peace deal, but Iran interfered and prevented the rebels from pursuing productive negotiations. These political clashes have consequences. Several million lives depend on timely food aid.

Eight Knowns

Known 1: According to the US State Department, Iran uses human trafficking to facilitate and fund its destabilizing activities around the globe. Iran may have used prostitution rings to recruit fighters for proxy wars. Regime intelligence and special operations agencies are also involved in drug trafficking. American and European security agencies have accused Iran of using drug-smuggling revenue to finance its disruption and terror operations.

Known 2: Smuggling warfare is an important operation in Yemen. Iranian smuggling warfare has kept Houthi fighters in the field. Most of the foreign aid for civilians in rebel-held areas passes through the port of Hodeida. The rebels, however, have expelled UN personnel tasked with inspecting aid shipments. The government claims that the rebels steal or divert aid shipments. They prevent UN officials from verifying that the aid is going to civilians, not Houthi fighters. In March 2015, Iran made a deal with the Shia rebels to modernize and upgrade Hodeida, but with the intervention of the Saudi-led coalition, that Iranian aid effort never got going.

Known 3: Like China, the Khomeinists spin a grandiose narrative of a return to Great Power status. They support that narrative with one of grievance. Iran's narrative of ancient imperial revival differs in content but not in form from China's (chapter three) and Russia's (chapter four). Sunni Muslim caliphate revivalists in Al Qaeda and the Islamic State use the same framework. The Khomeinist narrative mobilizes domestic and foreign Shia support for the regime's less-grandiose regional ventures and its global skull-duggery. From roughly 1500 BC to seventh century AD, Iran (in various guises) was a regional superpower. The 642 AD Arab Muslim defeat of the Sassanid Empire humiliated Iranians. In the thirteenth century, Mongols struck from the east and sacked Persia. Extended conflict with Ottoman Turks and Western states followed. Iranian revivalists recite a great litany of Western depredations, such as the British D'Arcy oil concession (1901), the formation of the insidious Anglo-Persian Oil Company (1909), and the 1953 coup backed by US and British intelligence agencies that toppled the democratically-elected Prime Minister Mohammad Mossadegh. Mossadegh made the mistake of nationalizing Iran's oil industry.

Known 4: Many senior Shia clerics are Quietists; they believe senior clergy should rarely become involved in government politics. They oppose "the vocal school" of Shia clerics, such as Ayatollah Khomeini and his followers. They offer a counter-narrative that threatens a fundamental regime narrative.

Known 5: "Divide and conquer" works well where division is the norm. For over three decades, former president Saleh encouraged tribal divisions in Yemen. He wanted to prevent the formation of tribal coalitions that might challenge him.

Known 6: Since the formation of the GCC in 1981, Saudi Arabia and the UAE have fought over council leadership. However, in Yemen they have concentrated on defeating the common enemy, Iran.

Known 7: From 1962 to 1967, Egypt intervened in the Yemeni civil war. Egyptian forces supported the secular Yemen Arab Republic, which was battling Shia tribesmen in northern Yemen. The tribesmen supported a former Yemeni monarch. Saudi Arabia and Jordan supported the royalists. About ten thousand Egyptian soldiers died in what is now called the North Yemen Civil War. Egypt was accused of using chemical weapons (phosgene, or mustard gas) against the tribesmen. Evidence for use in at least two attacks is substantial.

Known 8: The Obama administration's "Iran nuclear deal," the Joint Comprehensive Plan of Action, was not comprehensive. It had weak nuclear inspection and enforcement mechanisms. It also failed to penalize the Iranian regime's covert and overt violent trouble-making—a grievous flaw given Iran's violent behavior. In 1984, the US State Department put Iran on its list of state sponsors of terrorism. In March 2018, it was still on the terrorist list. In 2011, an Iranian operative was arrested before he could assassinate a Saudi diplomat in a Washington, D.C., restaurant. The Iranian operative intended to kill the diplomat with a bomb.

Three Unknowns

Unknown 1: Would a de-nuclearized North Korea sell its nuclear technology and, perhaps, weapons to Iran?

Unknown 2: Would sustained lower oil prices force the Iranian regime to retreat from more expensive troublemaking projects, such as in Yemen and Syria? Economic deterioration and regime corruption have ignited mass protests inside Iran. Since roughly 1995, this has been Iran's deep question: when will the Iranian people be willing to spill their own blood to confront the clerical dictatorship?

Unknown 3: How much of the Iranian economy is controlled by the IRGC and hardline senior Shia clerics? Saudi Arabia claims that Shia radicals control from fifty to sixty percent of Iran's economy. Corruption, repression, and meddling aggression have benefited the hardliners.

Tactical, Operational, and Strategic Complexities to Ponder

Complexity 1: Where does Yemen's water go? Traditionally, Yemen was the Arabian Peninsula's breadbasket. Annual monsoon rains brought water. However, food production in Yemen has declined. Nearly half of the water used by Yemen's agricultural sector goes to produce khat, an addictive plant that users chew—and chew and chew.

Complexity 2: From four hundred thousand to one million Iranians died in the Iran-Iraq War (1980–1988) that began when Iraqi dictator Saddam Hussein attacked Iran. Saddam thought Khomeini's new regime might fold. It didn't. The war, pitting Iranians against Arabs, became the deadliest modern Middle Eastern armed conflict. Iraqi Arabs are predominantly Shia; that didn't curb the bloodshed. The war hardened anti-Arab attitudes in Iran.

Anti-Arab attitudes existed before Islam. Shia Muslim Iran and Sunni Muslim Saudi Arabia are not only twenty-first century regional rivals and sectarian Muslim rivals, they are also ancient ethnic rivals—Iranian Aryans versus Arab Semites. Call the Gulf what you will; history circa 500 BC stirs violent passions in the Aryan-Arab collision. In pitiful Yemen, these ancient antagonists back opposing political and tribal factions. They also deploy their own forces, covertly and overtly.

Moreover, Iranian intrigues throughout the world have threatened both Sunni Muslim Saudi Arabia and Israel, both veterans of twentieth-century Arab-Israeli enmity. Truth be told, since 1979 they have had a common enemy: Iran's malign regime. In June 2015, Saudi Arabia and Israel publicly acknowledged they were discussing ways to combat the Khomeinists. Regarding 500 BC, the narrative starts with Genesis. Arabs claim descent from Ishmael, Abraham's son by his concubine Hagar. Jews claim descent from Abraham's wife, Sarah. In the deep text of Iranian narrative warfare in Iraq, Syria, Lebanon, Yemen, and North Africa, Shia Aryans (Iranians) battle ethnically inferior Sunni and Jewish Semites and their mongrel ethnic ally, America (also known as the Great Satan in Khomeinist propaganda). Shia Arabs? Well, those enlightened Semites help Iranian clerics advance the greater cause.

Three Military Scenarios

This list is meant to be illustrative of wars that Iranian meddling, agitation, and belligerence in Yemen or Saudi Arabia might encourage or escalate. The scenarios are speculations, not predictions.

1. **The Joint and Comprehensive Plan of Attack (a preemptive attack on Iranian nuclear facilities).** In 1982, Israeli aircraft attacked and destroyed Iraq's Osirak reactor, which Israel believed was part of an active Iraqi nuclear weapons program. If Iran obtains nuclear weapons, Israel and Saudi Arabia might launch air and missile attacks to destroy weapon storage sites and weapon delivery systems. The US might be involved.

2. **Hormuz/Bab el-Mandab Oil Choke-Point War.** Iran consistently threatens to close the Strait of Hormuz to oil-tanker traffic. An Iranian-controlled Yemen might threaten to close the Bab el-Mandab. Closing either one or both would amount to waging economic war on several US allies. Look for the US, the GCC coalition, and NATO to be involved in these conflicts.

3. **The War to Prevent Hezbollah Land South.** Saudi Arabia, Egypt, and Israel are concerned that an Iranian-controlled

Yemen would become another base for attacks throughout the region. In Lebanon, Hezbollah guerrillas are close to the Israeli border. Yemen is some distance from Egypt and Israel, but Iranian operatives can hide longer-range missiles in Yemen's remote areas. Essentially, this would be a continuation of the proxy war without conventional ground troops. Air strikes and raids would target Iranian training camps and weapon sites. Egypt and Israel could be involved. A variant: This war might follow and/or include an Israeli attack on Lebanon's Hezbollah Land North.

CHAPTER 6

CONGO

Anarchic Violence, Cyclic Intervention, and Mineral Wealth

The Democratic Republic of Congo does the world a sad but valuable service. Congo's hell of poverty, multifarious wars, ethnic antagonism, frail government institutions, porous borders, meddling neighbors, cyclical epidemics, and corrupt elites provide a one-stop shop example of the wicked conditions afflicting the globe's less-developed regions—sub-Saharan Africa in particular. Even more-developed states have (and often try to hide) these wicked conditions. Though its cultural, historical, demographic, and geographic contexts are vastly different from Congo's, pre-2011 Syria comes to mind. A faux stability imposed by police state terror masked Syria's explosive jumble of criminal elites, poverty, and ethnic and sectarian savagery. Some commentators call Congo a failed state. The flag and UN seat that Congo's wretched government possess is a façade, so "façade state" is a bit more accurate. Congo has never

Chapter Abbreviation Key

CENCO = National Episcopal Conference of Congo. Organization of Catholic Church bishops.

CENI = Independent National Electoral Commission in Congo. (Its independence is disputed.)

DRC = Democratic Republic of Congo

FARDC = French abbreviation for the Congolese Army—Forces armées de la république démocratique du Congo (Armed Forces of the Democratic Republic of Congo)

FIB or IBDE = Abbreviations for the UN's Congo peacekeeping combat brigade. Official name is Force Intervention Brigade. IBDE, for Intervention Brigade, is also used. The UN Security Council gave this unit a mandate to conduct "targeted offensive operations." That means the brigade engages in oxymoronic operations too blunt for gun-shy diplomats: "war-making peacekeeping."

IMF = International Monetary Fund

MONUC = United Nations Organization Mission in the Democratic Republic of Congo, a peacekeeping operation, 2000–2010

MONUSCO = United Nations Organization Stabilization Mission in the Democratic Republic of Congo, 2010–present (MONUC was renamed in 2010)

NGO = Non-governmental organization. The Red Cross is a secular NGO. The Catholic Church is a sectarian NGO.

ONUC = United Nations Operation in the Congo, the UN's first peacekeeping operation, 1960–1964 (see History)

UNHCR = United Nations High Commissioner for Refugees. The UN's refugee agency. Has a major presence in Central Africa.

WFP = World Food Program (Programme). International food-relief and nutrition assistance organization.

been a nation-state; it is an anarchic zone. Within the anarchic zone, armed actors clash with other armed actors and struggle to secure territorial or criminal fiefdoms. Some territorial fiefdoms are large, provincial in size, and—not surprisingly—similar geographically and demographically to pre-colonial and colonial-era tribal lands.

Other fiefs consist of neighborhoods or a single village protected by a local and usually tribal militia. Fiefs with valuable minerals are hotly contested. Meanwhile, Congo's elites battle among themselves, fighting for control of the capital, Kinshasa, and its government ministries, especially those with police and financial-regulatory power. The elite-ruled national government wages economic, diplomatic, and narrative warfare with global financial agencies (such as the IMF), medical aid and relief NGOs, donor nations (wealthy foreign powers), and international corporations. Why do donor nations, the IMF, and international corporations bother? They have many motives, including legitimate humanitarian concern. However, in Congo's hell cocktail, mineral fiefs are the critical reason. Certain areas within Congo's anarchic zone have the world's largest deposits of very valuable minerals. For example, high-tech electronic manufacturing processes require Congolese minerals such as cobalt and coltan (refined to produce tantalum). The vast majority of the world's less-developed nations are not blessed with such a bounty. However, both the desire to control those mineral deposits and the desire to obtain access to them have ignited or exacerbated wars within Congo.

Overview

In March 2018, as I completed this book, violent battles and raids were occurring in at least ten (possibly twelve) of Congo's twenty-six provinces. The firefights involved combat forces of varying sizes and varying degrees of training, discipline, and organization.

With an area of over 770,000 square miles, Congo is roughly the size of Western Europe. As a thought experiment, imagine the malign consequences if persistent, low-intensity warfare afflicted forty percent of Western Europe. At the very least, regional transportation would be difficult and the tourist industry would suffer.

Since the Congo War erupted (also called the First Congo War, 1996–1997), at one time or another every Congolese province has experienced anarchic violence. When anarchic violence erupts, unprotected civilians are uprooted or robbed, sometimes raped, often killed. Displaced people often die from exposure. This is a humanitarian and cultural disaster. The violence often destroys homes and other stores of personal wealth, such as crops, granaries, and businesses. The economic loss a region suffers may take years to replace. Corrupt or ill-trained government security forces provide civilians haphazard protection—a military-security issue that deals nation-builders psychological and information warfare defeats. The population has little or no faith in government institutions. Even areas of comparative calm are deeply affected by neighboring unrest and warfare as floods of refugees flee combat zones.

In these impossible circumstances, Congolese civilians, aid groups, and human rights organizations legitimately demand protection. Via cellphone, the world hears their pleas.

In 2000, responding belatedly to the Great Congo War (also called the Second Congo War, 1998–2003), the UN Security Council authorized the United Nations Mission in the Democratic Republic of Congo (MONUC). Year by year, the troop commitment increased, reaching twenty thousand in 2010.

In 2010, MONUC became MONUSCO (United Nations Organization Stabilization Mission in the Democratic Republic of Congo). The new name reflects a shift in UN policy, from peacekeeping to political stabilization. The word "stabilization" signaled that the UN would withdraw troops as Congo's security forces became strong enough to defend Congolese civilians.

Peacekeeping troops would provide a reassuring security presence but would increasingly focus on improving Congolese Army units and police units.

However, as of mid-2018, the Congolese Army has not improved to the point it can secure the country. Why?

Ethnic rivalries and poorly educated soldiers are the usual reasons, but they are also excuses. Complexity 1 addresses issue in the context of weak government institutions that remain weak. Many international observers believe that corrupt Congolese elites prefer weak government institutions; weakness makes the institutions easier to control and manipulate.

The Congolese Army's failure to become more professional and assume the burden of internal security specifically implicates Joseph Kabila. Kabila, president from 2001 to 2018, knew a weak, divided, and corrupt Congolese Army did not threaten his regime. That was especially important after he refused to relinquish his office when his term expired in December 2016 (see the following Relevant Geography and History). Rumor has it that Kabila spent military modernization funds on his loyal presidential guard and national police. The 2006 Congo constitution was based on the peace agreement that ended the Great Congo War. Limiting the president to two terms was a key component of that agreement. The constitution enshrined the two-term limit. The idea was to prevent a return to a "strong man" dictatorship like those of the multi-decade tyrants so common in Africa that colonial rule ended in the 1960s. At the bottom line, Kabila decided that his grip on power was more important than peace. To remain president or to retain power behind-the-scenes, he was willing to risk a bloody war that would result in another million dead.

By some estimates, UN peacekeeping and related efforts in Congo have cost twelve billion dollars since 2000. That is a major, sustained effort over an extended period of time.

Peace? In March 2018—the month with serious armed clashes in at least ten provinces—the UN reported that Congo's internal conflicts had put thirteen million people at physical risk. More than four-and-a-half million children are acutely malnourished (on the verge of starvation). Medical relief agencies reported that Congo's 2018 cholera epidemic was the worst outbreak since 2003. Despite the government's claims of ending warfare in the Kasai region, new violence was occurring. The Hema-versus-Lendu war in Ituri province was escalating.

Key Actors

Congo Government, Its Agencies and Security Forces: Nominally a federal republic, the government is really a strongman-type dictatorship backed by security forces.

Key Congolese Opposition Groups: Rassemblement (French for "rally") is the opposition's umbrella organization. The Union for Democracy and Social Progress and the People's Party for Reconstruction and Democracy are major opposition parties.

Catholic Church in Congo: Works with other NGOs and with aid and human rights organizations.

UN/MONUSCO: As of 2018, the UN's peacekeeping force is the most powerful army in Congo.

Donor Nations: Wealthier nations that provide aid and loans. The group is rather large and includes European Union member nations, Great Britain, Japan, Australia, India, Canada, and the US.

China: China has invested heavily in Katangan mineral resources and related enterprises.

Congo's Muscular Neighbors: Rwanda, Uganda, Angola, and Tanzania. The first three have authoritarian governments and reliable armies. Tanzania is a bit more relaxed but also has well-trained military.

Congo's Chaotic Neighbors: Anarchy, secessionists, ethnic conflict, economic rot, and elite authoritarianism afflict Burundi, South Sudan, the Central African Republic (CAR), Congo-Brazzaville (the Republic of the Congo), Cameroon, and Zambia. They are smaller versions of the Democratic Republic of the Congo.

Wild Cards

Mai Mai Militias: Individually they are wild cards. Collectively they are a huge problem. In Kiswahili, *mai* (*mayi*) means "water." Supposedly, Mai Mai fighters spray themselves with a magic potion to deflect bullets. One source says it refers to drinking potions. The term "Mai Mai" was supposed to indicate an autonomous militia organized to oppose imperialist or foreign (that is, non-Congolese) forces invading Congo. In fact, Laurent Kabila formed and supplied several Mai Mai militias in northern Katanga for the express purpose of opposing invading Rwandan forces. They were not fully autonomous.

Gecamines: Congo's state-owned mineral exploration and production company. Has financial and regulatory roles. A great company to bribe.

IMF: The macro-economic financial institution was founded in 1945 to foster international financial stability, trade, and economic modernization. May provide nations requesting economic aid— such as Congo—with advice and conditional loans. Loan conditions almost always involve economic reform. Congolese governments have been slow to reform.

International Mining Companies (Private and State-owned): Congo has vast mineral and elemental resources. A sample: uranium, copper, cobalt, tantalum, niobium, diamonds, gold, silver, tin, zinc, and manganese. (Tantalum is refined from coltan.)

TP Mazembe: Tout Puissant Mazembe, Congo's champion football (soccer) club. Beloved throughout Congo. Owned by opposition politician Moise Katumbi. Based in Lubumbashi, Katanga.

Radical Islamist Organizations: The Ugandan rebel group Allied Democratic Forces (ADF) has a limited but violent presence in eastern Congo. Congo and Uganda believe that Muslim extremists in the Middle East finance the ADF. The ADF may also be involved in gold smuggling.

Six Knowns (or, in Congo's Case, Highly Probables)

Known 1: In 2014, numerous media critics declared MONUSCO a failure. However, in 2004 other critics had declared MONUC an abject disaster. When compared to Congo 2004, Congo 2014 was more stable. In 2018, UN Department of Peacekeeping (DPKO) officials could make a strong case that regional (international) tensions related to internal Congolese warfare have been reduced. The UN's Force Intervention Brigade played a key role in reducing regional tensions in eastern Congo. But the overall effort has not produced a peaceful, prosperous Congo. Internal anarchic violence continues.

Known 2: Joseph Kabila's refusal to relinquish his office when his term ended in December 2016 exacerbated internal tensions and contributed to the anarchic violence. That fact leads to this speculation: Stirring violent crises may have been his goal, since some frightened people might choose to accept the devil they know. The "overstayer in chief" intentionally made the UN peacekeeping mission more difficult. How corrupt national and tribal leaders and corrupt economic elites aggravate local conflicts for personal gain receives limited attention. It is easy to report on customs officials demanding bribes at the Kinshasa airport. Cracking the Swiss bank accounts of the dictator and the army generals is a much tougher task.

Known 3: The UN's Force Intervention Brigade still has critics who argue that offensive mandates authorizing the "neutralization" of specific factions mean the UN has overtly chosen sides. When its peacekeepers enter a sovereign country with the mandate to attack a rebel faction, the UN loses more than credibility as a mediator. Come the next dirty war, the critics argue, peacekeeping forces will be met as invaders. Advocates of the offensive mandate convinced the UN that endless murder and mass rape by rogue militias do anything but promote peace. The offensive mandate got results. (See A Sampling of Events in Three Complex Internal Congolese Wars: the North and South Kivu section.)

Known 4: Congo's corrupt elites resist reform. The Kabila family provides an example. The Kabila clan has extensive mining interests (including gold, diamonds, cobalt, and copper). Joseph Kabila took control of the government after his father was assassinated in 2001.

Yes, a family business. He violated the constitution by remaining in office, and the constitution was both a peace treaty and a mechanism for political reform. Allegations are rampant that the Kabilas and their supporters have used those years of executive control to steal billions of dollars' worth of foreign aid and engage in illegal mining and exporting operations. There are grounds for criminal indictment by the International Criminal Court.

Known 5: Congolese courts are corrupt. (See Known 4.)

Known 6: Katanga province is wealthy enough and powerful enough to survive as a separate country. Katangan secessionists played a central role in the 1960 Congo crisis. In some respects (such as clout with the global economy), controlling Katanga's capital, Lubumbashi, is more important than controlling Kinshasa. Lubumbashi has rail links to both the Atlantic and Indian Oceans.

Three Unknowns

Unknown 1: MONUSCO fields by far the most powerful armed force in Congo. However, peacekeeping frustration and fatigue could lead to a withdrawal of UN peacekeepers. What would happen if UN military and police personnel withdraw?

Unknown 2: Possibly connected to Unknown 1. What will happen to Joseph Kabila's presidential guard when he is no longer officially president? Will the guard transfer its loyalty to the new chief executive or remain loyal to Kabila? The presidential guard has around twelve thousand personnel. It is the best-trained and best-armed Congolese military force in Congo. It could stage a Praetorian Guard–type coup. One scenario has Kabila claiming that a national crisis requires his return to office. Another scenario has a

Kabila proxy replacing him as president after "winning" a presidential election (which will be tagged by allegations of vote fraud and voter intimidation).

Unknown 3: Several opposition political leaders classify as elites, especially Moise Katumbi. He is very wealthy and has mining interests. Are these opposition leaders really interested in fundamental change in Congo's corrupt, predatory system? Will an elite replace an elite and essentially keep the corrupt system in place?

Relevant Geography and History

Over 250 ethnic groups inhabit Congo. The four largest groups— the Mongo, Luba, Kongo (Bakongo), and Mangbetu-Azande—make up about forty-five percent of the population. The Congo River, the country's major river, is named after the Bakongo people. Over 650 local languages and dialects are spoken in Congo. Lingala, a Congolese patois, is the language used by the Congolese Army and the closest thing to a national Congolese language. French and Swahili are also spoken.

Congo's people are eighty-five to ninety percent Christian. The population is over eighty-four million; in 2000, it was around fifty million. Agricultural development has not kept pace with expanding domestic food needs. About thirty million Congolese live in cities. Eleven million live in Kinshasa and its immediate environs. Brazzaville, the capital of the Republic of the Congo, is just across the Congo River from Kinshasa.

Congo's terrain varies greatly, from savannas and grasslands to mountains to tropical rainforests. About eighty percent of the country is forest and woodland. Though the majority of the country is tropical, the southern area suffers periodic droughts. The eastern highlands are somewhat cooler and wetter.

Congo has a central position and borders nine countries: Angola, Zambia, Tanzania, Burundi, Rwanda, Uganda, Sudan, Central African Republic, and Congo-Brazzaville (the Republic of the Congo, on the other side of the Congo River).

Relevant History Since 1960

1960: The UN Operation in the Congo (ONUC) deploys peacekeeping forces to Congo. This is the year Congo becomes independent and its Belgian colonialists depart. Then Katangan separatists rebel. The Katanga secessionists, led by Moise Tshombe, want their own country. Congo's government, led by Patrice Lumumba, claims Belgium is financing the separatists. As anarchic violence spread throughout Congo, the UN intervenes. (The Katangan separatists will surrender in 1963.)

1965: The Tshombe government falls. Mobutu Sese Seko, an army general, becomes dictator and declares himself president. He will head the government until 1997.

1977: Katangan separatists with ties to Tshombe's security forces attack Katanga from bases in Angola. They use the name National Front for the Liberation of the Congo (FNLC). France airlifts Moroccan troops to Congo to aid Mobutu. The invasion fails.

1978: Katangan separatists attack and seize the Katangan town of Kolwezi. French and Belgian paratroopers intervene, and the secessionists are defeated.

1980s: Congo's economy slowly disintegrates. Mobutu's "kleptocracy" (government based on theft and corruption) steals from foreign-aid donors and Congo's impoverished people.

1996–1997: Congo War/First Congo War: This conflict destroys Mobutu's regime. Hutu tribal radicals, the genocidaires of Rwanda's 1994 genocide, disrupted eastern Congo when they fled vengeful Tutsis. Mobutu's regime cannot cope. When Mobutu leaves Congo for cancer treatments in Europe, General Laurent Kabila rebels and attacks Mobutu's supporters. In late spring 1997, Kabila (father of Joseph Kabila) seizes Lubumbashi, Katanga. In May 1997, Kabila, with Rwandan allies, takes Kinshasa. Kabila declares himself president. The ill Mobutu flees Congo and dies in exile.

1998–2003: Great Congo War/Second Congo War: In July 1998, Laurent Kabila turns on his Rwandan and Ugandan allies. In August 1999, Banyamulenge Tutsis in the North Kivu province (next door to Rwanda) rebel. A Banyamulenge militia takes control of key towns in eastern Congo. The rebellion spreads. Rwanda intervenes. Kabila forces manage to retain control of Kinshasa and key Katangan cities and mines. A complex, multi-sided war emerges. Angola, Zimbabwe, and Namibia back Kabila. Uganda and Rwanda back the rebels. Fighters from Sudan, Libya, and Chad also enter Congo to support Kabila. Rwandan and Ugandan forces clash in eastern Congo.

February 2000: The UN authorizes a new peacekeeping operation, MONUC. The peacekeepers are supposed to monitor a ceasefire agreement, but warfare continues throughout Congo.

January 2001: Laurent Kabila is assassinated by one of his bodyguards.

2001: The anarchic warfare features mass murder, rape, and looting. Pockets of stability exist, some protected by resident militias.

2002: MONUC peacekeepers deploy in force. Zimbabwean, Angolan, and Namibian contingents withdraw. Tutsi fighters in eastern Congo begin to lay down arms. Congo and Uganda sign a peace agreement. Most warring parties sign what is called the Global and All-Inclusive Agreement.

July 2003: A transitional Congolese government is established. The fighting subsides. The war is over but the warfare isn't. Mai Mai militias plague Katanga. Hutu genocidaire FDLR fighters and Tutsi militias battle in the Kivus. Ugandan forces withdraw by late 2003.

2003–2011: UN peacekeeping operations continue. From 2004 to 2007, UN peacekeepers and the Congolese Army (FARDC) engage in heavy fighting with militia forces. There are incremental successes. But the FDLR and other vicious militias continue to operate. In 2011, Joseph Kabila is re-elected president. In 2006, Joseph Kabila is elected president. He defeats Jean-Pierre Bemba in a runoff election in October 2006.

2012–2013: Militia violence rises, particularly in eastern Congo.

March 2013: The UN Security Council approves the creation of the Force Intervention Brigade to fight armed groups in the eastern Congo. The FIB will be allowed to conduct "targeted offensive operations"—which is diplo-speak for offensive combat. Malawi, Tanzania, and South Africa will each provide an infantry battalion with 850 soldiers (2,550 soldiers total). The remaining authorized 519 troops will serve in three separate companies: an artillery battery, a special forces company, and a recon company.

December 19, 2016: Joseph Kabila's second term as president ends, but he refuses to leave office.

December 31, 2016: The December Accord (also called the Saint Sylvester agreement) maps out a peaceful political path for Kabila's exit. Congo's Catholic bishops mediate the negotiations. New elections are to be held in 2017—except those elections will not occur.

A Sampling of Events in Three Complex Internal Congolese Wars

Ituri Province

Ituri province has witnessed of some of Congo's worst fighting. An estimated sixty thousand people died between 1999 and 2007. Most were slain in what is called militia warfare. In 2008, about four million people lived in Ituri. Do the math. In eight years, one-and-a-half percent of the population was killed.

The Hema and Lendu tribes and their militias are responsible for some of the most hideous violence. The Hema are cattle raisers and herders (pastoralists). The Lendu, who are the dominant tribe in Ituri, are primarily farmers (agriculturalists). That is an age-old recipe for trouble; the pastoralists complain about the agriculturalists seizing their lands, and the agriculturalists object to pastoralist herds grazing on their farms. The Hema also consider themselves to be cousins of the Tutsis. The Lendus regard the Hutus as kin. Tutsi genocide committed by Rwandan Hutus in 1994 intensified the Hema-Lendu animosity.

In 2016, Hema-versus-Lendu violence once again flared. In 2017, it intensified. In early 2018, Hema militias attacked Lendu villages. By March an estimated fifty thousand Lendu had fled to Uganda.

North and South Kivu Provinces

The UN Force Intervention Brigade has targeted several rogue militias. In the Kivus it fought and defeated the M23 (March 23) rebel group. FIB actions against M23 began on August 22, 2013. By November 2013, M23 was shattered. In 2014, the brigade targeted and reduced the Democratic Forces for the Liberation of Rwanda (FDLR). The FDLR was founded by Rwandan Hutu genocidaires. FDLR splinter groups still operate in eastern Congo.

In 2017 and 2018, the FIB attacked the Ugandan rebel group Allied Democratic Forces–National Army for the Liberation of Uganda (ADF–NALU) which has bases in North Kivu. The ADF has links to Somalia's Islamist al-Shabaab organization.

In South Kivu, the FIB and other UN peacekeepers have fought Mai Mai militias operating along Congo's border with Burundi. The militias would attack and plunder defenseless towns.

Kasai

The conflict erupted in August 2016 when Kabila government forces killed a traditional local chief, Jean-Pierre Mpandi. Mpandi had come to Kasai to claim the title of *kamuina nsapu*, the traditional (customary) chief of a local Luba clan. Mpandi was a critic of Kabila. The Kabila government denied him the office and appointed a Kabila supporter to the position. Mpandi objected to government interference in tribal affairs and called on local citizens to resist. They did, and formed a militia named Kamuina Nsapu. Militia leaders accused Kabila of seeking unjust political domination. That accusation had resonance among other political and ethnic groups in Congo who oppose Kabila—especially after he refused to cede power when his presidential term ended in December 2016. The violence escalated and spread throughout the Kasai region (which is about the size of Germany). The region has five provinces: Kasai, Kasai-Central, Kasai-Oriental, Sankuru, and Lomami. By 2018, the death toll had exceeded six thousand. The UN high commissioner for refugees estimated the violence had displaced one-and-a-half million people.

Two Complexities

Complexity 1: Congolese elite prefer weak government institutions. Per the chapter overview, many informed observers believe corrupt Congolese elites want the key government institutions to remain weak so they can influence them and control them. Congo's corrupt elites play a game of divide and dominate. Congo, however, needs reliable, trained security forces. Infrastructure and industry need new investment. Economic decline must be stopped, and economic development fostered. Education programs focusing on literacy and small business are a requirement. Corrupt officials must be arrested and prosecuted. But to do that would require strong and honest legal government ministries and legal institutions.

Complexity 2: Third-Term President Club: Rwanda, Burundi, and the Republic of the Congo (Congo-Brazzaville), now have presidents who either changed or violated national constitutions in order to seek a third term and retain power. Respectively, they are Paul Kagame, Pierre Nkurunziza, and Denis Sassou Nguesso. Nkurunziza's action sparked stiff resistance in Burundi.

Foreign-Power Strategic Goals and Military, Economic, and Diplomatic Operations
United Nations

A UN Operational Cocktail Analysis: The UN has studied MONUC and MONUSCO and concluded that future peacekeeping missions must seek political solutions. Military elements of an operation should not be separated from police-security and civilian operations. Instead of relying just on random troop contingents supplied by UN members, the UN wants soldiers whose skills the mission requires. The UN wants to create "peace operations packages" tailored to specific local conditions. The UN peacekeeping office concluded that rapid reaction makes a difference. Get there first with the most. As for the Force Intervention Brigade, it was a tactical and operational military success in Congo. However, there will be future operations in which the UN will serve best as a neutral arbiter.

China

Strategic Goal in Congo: Assure access to critical minerals.

Economic Operation to Support Strategic Goal: Chinese companies own several dozen processing plants in Katanga.

A Diplomatic-Economic Operation: In 2007, China agreed to build infrastructure in the Congo in exchange for mining concessions. The agreement was valued at nine billion dollars.

China's Cobalt Appetite: In 2016, the world produced an estimated 123,000 tons of cobalt, and fifty-seven percent of that came from Congo. Congo is also one of the world's top copper producers. Cobalt has many uses, but it is critical in the production of rechargeable lithium-ion batteries, the type used to power mobile digital devices and electric vehicles. It takes about twenty-two pounds of cobalt to manufacture an electric car battery. China builds millions of electric vehicles, especially electric cars.

Congo Economic-Diplomatic Operation Affecting China: The Congolese government has increased taxes on mining companies and raised royalty rates on strategic minerals—such as cobalt.

United States

Strategic Goal: Political stability in Central Africa. Given Congo's geographic centrality, stabilizing it advances this goal.

Great-Power Competition: The US is increasingly worried about Chinese port construction and transportation construction projects.

Strategic Military-Diplomatic Initiative: The US established African Command (AFRICOM) to provide military training assistance and advisers to African countries. This military-diplomatic initiative makes the statement that the US learned from 9/11 that it must be involved in the world's "chaotic corners" used by international terrorists as bases. AFRICOM works closely with the State Department and US aid agencies.

Military, Economic, and Diplomatic Operations: Operationally, the US prefers to work with and through African partners. In fact, that's the narrative—America works with partners. The US has a long-term training-assistance relationship with Uganda. Great Britain works closely with Kenya.

Military, Diplomatic, and Narrative Operational Failure: In 2010, the US military helped train Congo's 391st Commando Battalion. That military-diplomatic effort backfired. In 2013, the unit was accused of committing numerous crimes in North Kivu province in 2012. The crimes included looting and mass rape.

Diplomatic and Military Scenarios

The following is an illustrative list. These scenarios are speculations, not predictions.

1. **Call It Peace:** A peaceful transition in which the Kabila clique cedes power would rate as a UN success. But attempts to retain behind-the-scenes power would be met with resistance. How much resistance? That is another unknown.

2. **Roll the Ball Forward:** International peacekeepers continue to occupy Congo in order to buy time to create a capable Congolese Army and responsible police force. The peacekeepers will try to manage tribal agitation and opposition-group demands for more power sharing. The peacekeepers will conduct security operations to contain the turmoil.

3. **The Congo Cauldron Explodes:** Call it Kasai writ large. What would happen if serious armed violence spreads to all twenty-six Congolese provinces? Will foreign peacekeepers withdraw from the cauldron or reinforce? What would happen if a common enemy or common cause united several armed dissident groups within Congo? Will another Congo-wide civil war erupt? A disputed election could serve as a unifying event. The provincial wars, however, might remain discrete. Congolese political parties align fairly well with tribes or tribal groups. If election disputes lead to bloodletting, a tribal war could be a brick bashing or knife wound away.

4. **The Great Central African Spillover War:** South Sudan is a war zone, Burundi has a simmering civil war, the CAR is a fragmented tragedy, Cameroon is a land divided, and Zambia is no threat. However, Angola, Rwanda, and Uganda have

comparatively strong governments and well-trained military forces. All three entered Congo during Congo's civil wars. Would they intervene again if Congolese violence threatened their security? Uganda swears its military will never again plunder Congo—oh, but that Ituri gold! Rwandan Tutsis demand protection for Congolese Tutsis (the Banyamulenge). If the eastern Congo descends to utter chaos, would Rwandan "peacekeepers" secure a Banyamulenge-land buffer state?

5. **Great Congo War Redux:** Combine Scenarios 2 and 3.

6. **Katanga Will Rise Again:** Katanga isn't the only province ripe for secession. North Kivu and Bas Congo (western Congo) also have secessionist movements.

CONCLUSION

"**W**ell, ma'am, it's quite a hazardous form of peace."
In 1990, the reply I gave my utopian inquisitor succinctly described anxious, edgy, and armed conditions threatening hundreds of millions of human beings around the world.

A brief remembrance of three decades past: Throughout 1990, Turkish security forces and Kurdistan Workers' Party (PKK) rebels skirmished in a "war zone" along Turkey's southeastern border with Saddam's Iraq. In May 1990, Tuareg rebels attacked government forces in Mali and Niger. Several rebellions had occurred since the 1970s, but this one led to mutual accusations of mass atrocity. In October 1990, two months after Saddam Hussein invaded Kuwait (an attack that generated intense global media interest), a Tutsi rebel group invaded Rwanda. Radical Rwandan Hutus would later use this attack to justify their 1994 attacks on Tutsis—the ones that led to genocide.

As they occurred, the Tuareg, Rwandan, and Kurdish wars received minimal international news coverage. A couple of Western sectarian relief organizations reported on Rwanda as did Agence France-Presse and Reuters. AFP and Reuters reported on the Tuareg attacks. European wire services and Turkish newspapers covered the PKK war. Remember, in 1990 the Cold War hadn't fully expired. Kremlin tentacles touched the Kurdistan Workers' Party. An avowed Marxist organization was waging a separatist war within Turkey, a NATO country. Since the Turkish government had the firepower to kill Marxist insurgents by the hundreds, the war didn't provoke calamity headlines. However, senior leaders in Ankara and other NATO capitals knew that to end the insurgency, Turkey would have to secure the political and cultural rights of Turkish citizens who happened to be ethnic Kurds.

As we move through 2019 to 2020 and beyond, count the "heres" and "theres" where the hazardous peace holds as lucky.

This book has explored five case studies, each with political, security, and economic features that war and peace wagers will confront throughout the rest of the century. I have three thoughts to offer: (1) Wars such as Yemen's in which an outside power (Iran) benefits from seeding violence but successfully avoids direct punishment are very hard to resolve. (2) War is chaotic—non-linear, to employ the buzzword. In a particular war, actor interests are always "unbalanced"; moreover, their interests can change as time passes— war is a wicked problem. An actor's will to endure and win will vary. In the midst of a war, it is very difficult to determine which actors possess the will to win. Emotions and passions matter; however, they can be manipulated. So don't let the chaos, shifting interests, verbiage, what-ifs, and unknowns frighten you. Productive economic systems and competent military systems matter. So does adaptable leadership.

Thought 3 is an old thought recast: A war doesn't end when generals and diplomats sign documents and the UN issues a Security Council "amen."

How people involved in a war perceive on-the-ground conditions that are relevant to them fundamentally shapes a war's intensity and duration. Perceptions are no more static than on-the-ground conditions.

This is why the beginning of the end of a war requires assessing and addressing specific conditions in time.

How specific? Given the pervasiveness of cellphones with cameras, in many cases the knowledge must be street-specific.

Here's an exercise for would-be peace wagers. Go for a meandering walk in Nairobi, Khobar, Kabul, Kampala, Jakarta, Baghdad, Panama City, Londonistan, or the mess Americans call Chicago.

Walk, don't take a cab or bus. See the area, breathe it, touch it, *risk it.*

Did you survive? Did you have a police escort, or perhaps an infantry platoon with an armed drone overwatching you? Or did you walk alone?

Just remember this: Politics continue after the shooting stops.

RESOURCES

The "deep resource" for this book is the *Quick and Dirty Guide to War* book series I co-authored with James F. Dunnigan. The first edition came out in 1985. Subsequent editions (1986 trade paperback, 1992, 1996, 2008) always added new material. Some conflicts received less emphasis in later editions or disappeared altogether. For example, Spain's internal struggle with Catalan nationalism rated a chapter in the first edition; in subsequent editions it rated a paragraph. Alas, Catalonia separatism became a major European political issue in 2017.

However, the basic histories of major nations like Russia, China, and Iran are oft-told tales. This book relies on several history summaries found in *A Quick and Dirty Guide to War* 1996 Edition (William Morrow) and *A Quick and Dirty Guide to War* 2008 Edition (Paladin Press). Both editions are now out of print. The Korea, China, Iran, and Congo historical summaries draw on the history sections of both the 1996 and 2008 editions. The Russia Cold War-era material draws on the 1996 edition.

Qiao's and Wang's "Unrestricted Warfare" is another essential resource and is widely quoted, particularly in the Introduction and Chapter one.

The CIA World Factbook (online edition) provided most of the economic and demographic data. Some data came from *StrategyPage.com* posts, assessments and articles.

I made extensive use of *StrategyPage.com*'s "Wars Around the World" posts for historical information from 2000 on. This link leads to the "Wars Around the World" section's introduction page: https://www.strategypage.com/qnd/default.aspx.

James F. Dunnigan (Jim) has been the editor for *StrategyPage* since the website went online in 1999. Jim's beat includes Yemen. The timeline in the Yemen chapter draws heavily on Jim's Yemen-related posts from 2004 to 2018 and from material in various *A Quick and Dirty Guide to War* editions. *StrategyPage*'s current online Yemen archive starts in 2010. Pre-2010 Yemen data appears in Potential Hotspots posts, semi-annual wars updates, the Terrorism section (the October 2000 attack on the USS *Cole* occurred in the Yemeni port of Aden), and other Middle East wars sections. One Hotspot report from February 2006 on Yemen's Shia rebellion and a backgrounder on Yemen Jim wrote made my subsequent survey of news reports from 2004 to 2009 an easy task. I began assembling that timeline in October 2017.

This is old news for researchers, but initial incident reports are always incomplete and many are totally wrong. This is true for natural disasters and violent crime, but it's especially true for warfare. But "if it bleeds it leads" guides the news business.

Still, given time, the best news services eventually correct and update inaccurate reports. AFP, Reuters, and BBC "wire service" reports and UN summaries of events were key 2004–2009 resources. In 2015 and 2016, *Al Jazeera* published several solid in-depth reports on Yemen; *Al Jazeera* often used International Crisis Group (ICG) resources. I didn't use any *Al Jazeera* reports per se, but they supported other sources. ICG definitely appears in this resource list.

I found errors in *StrategyPage* updates—and newer updates adding more accurate data. However, *StrategyPage* updates aren't news; they are "a second brush at history"—assessments based on multiple sources. An update often appears weeks (occasionally, months) after an incident. Several think tanks do this in a more formal fashion than *StrategyPage*'s garage band. Jamestown Foundation "Briefs" are a first-class example (visit *Jamestown.org*).

In 2001, I began covering Congo and Central Africa for *StrategyPage*. I learned that developmental aid, humanitarian aid, and religious/sectarian organization websites are superior resources. These websites provided material for Yemen and Congo. Humanitarian aid organizations were a resource for Russia and Ukraine.

I took material from over ninety newspaper columns and articles I wrote from 1994 to 2018, far too many to list in any sensible resources section. The "creeping war of aggression" in the Russia–Ukraine chapter came from a column written in 1991 about Serbia's attack on Dubrovnik. The eleven Creators Syndicate columns I've listed as resources are exemplary and are still available online in the *StrategyPage* archive. Each book chapter has two related columns. The Trump administration diplomatic timeline in the Korea chapter uses material that originally appeared in essays I wrote for *The New York Observer* from March 2017 to March 2018. The March 2017 online *Observer* article appears on the Resource list. It has several of the quotes by former Secretary of State Rex Tillerson which appear in Chapter two. (Online it links to other sources.) I summarized the *Observer* material in a Creators column published May 1, 2018 (see the Resource List for the *StrategyPage* link). As for column Number

11, titled "What's Keeping Donald Rumsfeld Up At Night?" dated January 23, 2001, I include it as a warning. Its lede, written nine months before Al Qaeda's 9-11 attacks, has an *ex post facto* chill:

During his Senate confirmation hearings, Secretary of Defense Donald Rumsfeld was asked if he could name "one thing" that "kept him up at night" more than any other specific threat, terror, or trouble the Pentagon confronts.

Rumsfeld's answer was "intelligence."

In the defense business you never know enough and what you don't know will kill you.

REFERENCES

Al-Nidawi, Omar. 2017. "An Iranian Land Bridge Is Not the End of the World." Chemical Weapons in the Middle East - The Washington Institute for Near East Policy. The Washington Institute. October 16. http://www.washingtoninstitute.org/fikraforum/view/an-iranian-land-bridge-is-not-the-end-of-the-world.

Alterman, Jon B., ed. 2012. *Gulf Kaleidoscope: Reflections on the Iranian Challenge*. Washington, DC: Center for Strategic and International Studies.

Anderson, Jordan. 2017. "Old Tricks: DRC President Manoeuvres to Extend Rule." *Jane's Intelligence Review*, November 2017.

Ardemagni, Eleonora. 2017. "UAE-Backed Militias Maximize Yemen's Fragmentation." *IAI Istituto Affari Internazionali*. Istituto Affari Internazionali. September 4. http://www.iai.it/en/pubblicazioni/uae-backed-militias-maximize-yemens-fragmentation.

Ash, Timothy, Janet Frederica Gunn, John Iough, Lutsevych Orysia, James Nixey, James Sherr, and Kataryna Wolczuk. 2017. *The Struggle for Ukraine*. London: Royal Institute of International Affairs.

Bahgat, Gawdat. 2008. "United States-Iranian Relations: The Terrorism Challenge." *Parameters*, December 22, 2008.

Bahgat, Gawdat. 2008. "United States-Iranian Relations: The Terrorism Challenge." *Parameters*, December 22, 2008.

Bay, Austin. 2018. "On Point: The Ayatollahs' Brittle Regime Confronts A New Iranian Revolt." StrategyPage. StrategyPage. January 3, 2018. https://www.strategypage.com/on_point/20180103223613.aspx.

Bay, Austin. 2018. "On Point: China's Emperor Xi Rides The Tiananmen Tiger." StrategyPage. StrategyPage. February 27, 2018. https://www.strategypage.com/on_point/20180227232359.aspx.

Bay, Austin. 2016. "On Point: Congo's Crooked President Risks A New Civil War." StrategyPage. StrategyPage. November 1, 2016. https://www.strategypage.com/on_point/2016110122326.aspx.

Bay, Austin. 2003. "On Point: Congo Tragedy." StrategyPage. StrategyPage. July 16, 2003. https://www.strategypage.com/on_point/20030716.aspx.

Bay, Austin. 2017. "On Point: Congo's Vicious Kasai War Could Reignite The Great Congo War." StrategyPage. StrategyPage. August 9, 2017. https://www.strategypage.com/on_point/20170912233334.aspx.

Bay, Austin. 2016. "On Point: Korean Kaesong Experiment Shows Limits of Soft Power." StrategyPage. StrategyPage. February 16, 2016. https://www.strategypage.com/on_point/20160216222240.aspx.

Bay, Austin. 2017. "On Point: Russia's Probe in Ukraine Targets the Trump Administration." StrategyPage. StrategyPage. January 31, 2017. https://www.strategypage.com/on_point/20170131225224.aspx.

Bay, Austin. 2018. "On Point: The Trump Administration's Korea Diplomacy Timeline." StrategyPage. StrategyPage. May 1, 2018. https://www.strategypage.com/on_point/20180501225156.aspx.

Bay, Austin. 2004. "On Point: Ukraine and the Russian Wish to Return to Super-Power Status." StrategyPage. StrategyPage. November 30, 2004. https://www.strategypage.com/on_point/20041130.aspx.

Bay, Austin. 2017. "On Point: Wars Where Starvation Is a Weapon." StrategyPage. StrategyPage. June 13, 2017. https://www.strategypage.com/on_point/20170613223324.aspx.

Bay, Austin. 2001. "On Point: What's Keeping Donald Rumsfeld Up Late At Night?" StrategyPage. StrategyPage. January 23, 2001. https://www.strategypage.com/on_point/20010205.aspx.

Bay, Austin. 2017. "Rex Tillerson: North Korea Threat Is Imminent, Strategic Patience Is Over." *The New York Observer*. March 23, 2017. https://observer.com/2017/03/rex-tillerson-north-korea-threat-strategic-patience/

Biscop, Sven. 2017. "The Great Powers Have Their Ways." Issue brief. *The Great Powers Have Their Ways*. Brussels: Egmont Institute.

Bouchat, Clarence J. 2014. *The Paracel Islands and U.S. Interests and Approaches in the South China Sea*. Carlisle, PA: Strategic Studies Institute and U.S. Army War College Press.

Breen, Michael Geltzer, and Joshua A. 2011. "Asymmetric Strategies as Strategies of the Strong." *Parameters*, March 22, 2011.

Brown, David E. 2012. *Hidden Dragon, Crouching Lion: How Chinas Advance in Africa Is Underestimated and Africas Potential Underappreciated*. Carlisle, PA: Strategic Studies Institute, U.S. Army War College.

Cammaert, Patrick. 2013. "The UN Intervention Brigade in the Democratic Republic of the Congo." Issue brief. *The UN Intervention Brigade in the Democratic Republic of the Congo*. New York, NY: International Peace Institute.

Cathcart, Adam. 2017. "Tigers in the Haze: Chinese Troops on the Border with North Korea in the 'April Crisis.'" *China Brief*, October 20, 2017.

"China v the Rest." 2016. *The Economist*. The Economist Newspaper. March 26. https://www.economist.com/news/asia/21695565-sea -becomes-more-militarised-risks-conflict-grow-china-v-rest.

"Congo's War Was Bloody. It May Be about to Start Again." 2018. *The Economist. The Economist Newspaper*. February 15. https://www. economist.com/news/briefing/21737021-president-joseph-kabi-la-seventh-year-five-year-term-he-struggling-hold.

Cook, Nicholas. *Sub-Saharan Africa: Key Issues, Challenges, and U.S. Responses*. CRS Report No. R42618. Washington, DC: Congressional Research Service, 2012. https://fas.org/sgp/crs/row/R42618.pdf.

Cordesman, Anthony. 2018. "The Crisis in Iran: What Now?" Rep. Washington, DC: Center for Strategic and International Studies.

Cordesman, Anthony. 2018. "The Other Side of the North Korean Threat: Looking Beyond Its Nuclear Weapons and ICBMs." Washington, DC: Center for Strategic and International Studies.

Corn, Tony. 2018. "Grand Strategy with Chinese Characteristics." *Small Wars Journal.* Small Wars Foundation. Accessed August 6. http://smallwarsjournal.com/jrnl/art/grand-strategy-with-chinese-characteristics.

Corum, James S. 2013. *The Security Concerns of the Baltic States as NATO Allies.* Carlisle, PA: Strategic Studies Institute and U.S. Army War College Press.

"Countering Iranian Expansion in Syria." 2017. Rep. *Countering Iranian Expansion in Syria.* Washington, DC: Jewish Institute for National Security of America.

Dalton, Melissa. 2016. "Defeating the Iranian Threat Network: Options for Countering Iranian Proxies." Rep. *Defeating the Iranian Threat Network: Options for Countering Iranian Proxies.* Washington, DC: Center for Strategic and International Studies.

"Discord in Yemen's North Could Be a Chance for Peace." 2017. Issue brief. *Discord in Yemen's North Could Be a Chance for Peace.* Brussels: International Crisis Group.

Doshi, Rush. 2017. "Analysis | Xi Jinping Just Made It Clear Where China's Foreign Policy Is Headed." *The Washington Post.* WP Company. October 25. https://www.washingtonpost.com/news/monkey-cage/wp/2017/10/25/xi-jinping-just-made-it-clear-where-chinas-foreign-policy-is-headed/?utm_term=.29ae09528e09.

Dubik, James, and Nic Vincent. 2018. "America's Global Competitions: The Gray Zone in Context." Rep. *America's Global Competitions: The Gray Zone in Context.* Washington, DC: Institute for the Study of War.

Epple, Angelika, and Kirsten Kramer. 2016. "Globalization, Imagination, Social Space: The Making of Geopolitical Imaginaries." *Forum for Inter-American Research*9 (1): 41–63.

Fravel, M. Taylor. 2017. "Shifts in Warfare and Party Unity: Explaining China's Changes in Military Strategy." *International Security*42 (3): 37–83.

Fulton, Will, Joseph Holliday, and Sam Wyer. 2013. "Iranian Strategy in Syria." Rep. *Iranian Strategy in Syria.* Washington, DC: American Enterprise Institute's Critical Threats Project.

Giles, Keir. 2017. *The Turning Point for Russian Foreign Policy.* Carlisle, PA: Strategic Studies Institute and U.S. Army War College Press.

Gopalaswamy, Bharath, and Robert Manning. 2017. "The Sino-Indian Clash and the New Geopolitics of the Indo-Pacific." Rep. *The Sino-Indian Clash and the New Geopolitics of the Indo-Pacific.* Washington, DC: Atlantic Council.

Gray, Colin S. 2006. *Recognizing and Understanding Revolutionary Change in Warfare: the Sovereignty of Context.* Carlisle Barracks, PA: Strategic Studies Institute, U.S. Army War College.

Gray, Colin S. 2012. *Categorical Confusion?: the Strategic Implications of Recognizing Challenges Either as Irregular or Traditional.* Carlisle, PA: Strategic Studies Institute, U.S. Army War College.

Gregory, Paul Roderick. 2014. "Is Putin's New Type Of War In Ukraine Failing?" *RealClearWorld*. RealClear Media Group. April 29. https://www.realclearworld.com/blog/2014/04/is_putins_new_type_of_war_in_ukraine_failing_110467.html.

Holslag, Jonathan. 2009. "Chinas Africa Safari: On the Trail of Beijings Expansion in Africa." *Parameters*, 2009.

Huang, Paul An-hao. 2010. *The Maritime Strategy of China in the Asia-Pacific Region: Origins, Development and Impact*. Lewiston, NY: Mellen.

"A Huthi Missile, a Saudi Purge and a Lebanese Resignation Shake the Middle East." 2017. Rep. *A Huthi Missile, a Saudi Purge and a Lebanese Resignation Shake the Middle East*. International Crisis Group.

Joscelyn, Thomas, and Bill Roggio. 2017. "Analysis: CIA Releases Massive Trove of Osama Bin Laden's Files." FDD's Long War Journal. Public Multimedia Inc. November 1. https://www.longwarjournal.org/archives/2017/11/analysis-cia-releases-massive-trove-of-osama-bin-ladens-files.php.

Kan, Paul Rexton., Bruce E. Bechtol, and Robert M. Collins. 2010. *Criminal Sovereignty: Understanding North Koreas Illicit International Activities*. Carlisle, PA: Strategic Studies Institute, U.S. Army War College.

Katz, David J. 2017. "Waging Financial Warfare: Why and How." *Parameters*, 2017.

Kelly, David. 2018. "Seven Chinas: A Policy Framework." Rep. *Seven Chinas: A Policy Framework*. Washington, DC: Center for Strategic and International Studies.

Krieg, Andreas, and Jean Marc Rickli. 2018. "Surrogate Warfare: the Art of War in the 21st Century?" Taylor & Francis. *Defense Studies Journal*. January 21. https://www.tandfonline.com/doi/full/10.1080/14702436.2018.1429218.

Lamothe, Dan, and Carol Morello. 2017. "Securing North Korean Nuclear Sites Would Require a Ground Invasion, Pentagon Says." *The Washington Post*. WP Company. November 4, 2017. https://www.washingtonpost.com/world/national-security/securing-north-korean-nuclear-sites-would-require-a-ground-invasion-pentagon-says/2017/11/04/32d5f6fa-c0cf-11e7-97d9-bdab5a0ab381_story.html?utm_term=.726540d040c4.

Lebedev, Alexander, and Vladislav Inozemtsev. 2014. "Grappling With Graft." Foreign Affairs. *Foreign Affairs Magazine*. October 23. http://ww.foreignaffairs.com/articles/142280/alexander-lebedev-and-vladislav-inozemtsev/grappling-with-graft.

Liang, Qiao, and Wang Xiangsui. 1999. *Unrestricted Warfare*. Beijing: PLA Literature and Arts Publishing House Arts.

Meet the Press- October 24, 1999 Program. NBC's Tim Russert interviews Donald Trump on the North Korean threat. See: https://www.youtube.com/watch?v=G_IG07XhT3k This is the entire interview. The North Korea segment begins at 8:28.

Miller, Benjamin. 2017. "How Iran Became the Dominant Power in the Middle East." Rep. *How Iran Became the Dominant Power in the Middle East*. Perspectives Papers. Ramat Gan, Israel: The Begin-Sadat Center for Strategic Studies.

Moghadam, Assaf. 2017. "Marriage of Convenience: The Evolution of Iran and Al-Qa`Ida's Tactical Cooperation." *CTC Sentinel*, April 2017.

Monaghan, Andrew. 2015. "The 'War' in Russia's 'Hybrid Warfare.'" *Parameters*, 2015.

Nantulya, Paul. 2017. "A Medley of Armed Groups Play on Congo's Crisis." *ReliefWeb*. United Nations Office for the Coordination of Humanitarian Affairs. September 25. https://reliefweb.int/report/democratic-republic-congo/medley-armed-groups-play-congo-s-crisis.

O'Rourke, Ronald. *Maritime Territorial and Exclusive Economic Zone (EEZ) Disputes Involving China: Issues for Congress*. CRS Report No. R42784. Washington, DC: 2017. https://fas.org/sgp/crs/row/R42784.pdf

Office of Ocean and Polar Affairs, Kevin Baumert, and Brian Melchior. 2014. *Limits in the Seas—China: Maritime Claims in the South China Sea. Limits in the Seas—China: Maritime Claims in the South China Sea.*

Oxford English Dictionary. On line. Definition of "war." https://en.oxforddictionaries.com/definition/war

Parmar, Inderjeet. 2018. "The U.S.-Led Liberal Order: Imperialism By Another Name?" *International Affairs*94 (1): 151–72.

Person, James, ed. 2009. "Limits of the 'Lips and Teeth' Alliance: New Evidence on Sino-DPRK Relations, 1955-1984." Rep. *Limits of the "Lips and Teeth" Alliance: New Evidence on Sino-DPRK Relations, 1955-1984.* Washington, DC: Woodrow Wilson International Center for Scholars.

Petrarch, Francesco. *The Solitary Life* (or *Life of Solitude);* "the five enemies of peace" as quoted at Wikiquote, *https://p.curd.io/ en.wikiquote.org/wiki/Petrarch.*

Rachman, Gideon. 2017. "An Assertive China Challenges the West." *Financial Times.* Financial Times. October 23. https:// www.ft.com/content/d3fb6be8-b7d1-11e7-8c12-56617 83e5589?mhq5j=e6?segmentId.

Raska, Michael. 2017. "China and the 'Three Warfares.'" The Diplomat. The Diplomat. July 18. http://thediplomat.com/2015/12/ hybrid-warfare-with-chinese-characteristics-2/.

"Record of North Korea's Major Conventional Provocations since 1960s." 2010. Washington, DC: Center. Center for Strategic and International Studies.

Salisbury, Peter. 2018. "Yemen's Southern Powder Keg." Rep. *Yemen's Southern Powder Keg.* London, England: Chatham House.

Scobell, Andrew, and Larry M. Wortzel. 2006. *Shaping Chinas Security Environment: the Role of the Peoples Liberation Army.* Carlisle Barracks, PA: Strategic Studies Institute, U.S. Army War College.

Stronski, Paul, and Richard Sokolsky. 2017. "The Return of Global Russia: An Analytical Framework." Rep. *The Return of Global Russia: An Analytical Framework.* Washington, DC: Carnegie Endowment for International Peace.

Sunzi, and J. H. Huang. 1993. *The Art of War: the New Translation.* New York: Quill.

Szechenyi, Nicholas, ed., "China's Maritime Silk Road;" CSIS, March 2017. (PDF)

Szechenyi, Nicholas, ed. 2018. "China's Maritime Silk Road: Strategic and Economic Implications for the Indo-Pacific Region." Rep. *China's Maritime Silk Road: Strategic and Economic Implications for the Indo-Pacific Region.* Washington, DC: Center for Strategic and International Studies.

Terrill, W. Andrew. 2011. *The Conflicts in Yemen and U.S. National Security.* Carlisle, PA: Strategic Studies Institute, U.S. Army War College.

Tenzin, Palmo. 2015. "China, India and Water Across the Himalayas." *The National Interest.* The Center for the National Interest. August 3. http://nationalinterest.org/blog/the-buzz/what-could-start-war-between-india-china-13447.

"Time for Concerted Action in DR Congo." 2017. Issue brief. *Time for Concerted Action in DR Congo.* Nairobi/Brussels: International Crisis Group.

Wang, Guigo, and Priscilla Leung. 1998. "One Country, Two Systems: Theory Into Practice." *Pacific Rim Law & Policy Journal*, March, 280–321.

Weitz, Richard. 2017. *Promoting U.S.-Indian Defense Cooperation: Opportunities and Obstacles.* Carlisle, PA: Strategic Studies Institute and U.S. Army War College Press.

Whitehouse, Sheldon. 2017. "An Integrated Approach to the Himalayas: Report of the Working Group on the Himalayan Region." *Hudson Institute.* Speech presented at the South and Central Asia Program, October 31. https://www.hudson.org/

events/1482-an-integrated-approach-to-the-himalayas-report-of-the-working-group-on-the-himalayan-region102017.

Wood, Andrew. 2019. "Putin and Russia in 2018–24: What Next?" Rep. *Putin and Russian in 2018-24: What Next?* London, England: Chatham House.

"The World Factbook." 2016. Central Intelligence Agency. Central Intelligence Agency. April 1, 2016. https://www.cia.gov/library/publications/the-world-factbook/.

Xu, Xiang, and Alice Siqi Han. 2018. "Will China Collapse: A Review, Assessment and Outlook." Working paper. *Will China Collapse: A Review, Assessment and Outlook.* Stanford, CA: Hoover Institution Economics Working Papers.

ACKNOWLEDGMENTS

The following people deserve a thank-you for helping me complete *Cocktails from Hell*. Jim Dunnigan, Al Nofi, and Dan Masterson at StrategyPage.com, as well as Bradley Gernand (Institute for Defense Analysis), Paul Hlavinka, Michael Ledeen, Rick Runde, and Larry Wortzel provided advice and research assistance. Dan Masterson and my daughter, Annabelle Bay, provided clutch information technology assistance. In early March 2017, my editors at *The New York Observer*, Kelsey Smith and Merin Curotto, agreed North Korea's nuclear threat was a ripe topic and encouraged me to cover it in detail as the year progressed. As this book's publication deadlines approached, by Creators Syndicate editor, Maddy Hutchison, let my weekly column deadline slide a bit—and I sincerely appreciate it. I appreciate the support and patience of my literary agent, Laura Blake Peterson of Curtis Brown Ltd. Likewise, I appreciate the aid and perceptiveness of David Bernstein, the steadfastly encouraging fellow who edited this book.